Woman Alone:
CONFIDENT AND CREATIVE

Woman Alone:
CONFIDENT AND CREATIVE

Sarah Frances Anders

Broadman Press, Nashville, Tennessee

© Copyright 1976 • Broadman Press.
All rights reserved.

4252–39
ISBN: 0-8054-5239-7

Subject headings: SINGLE WOMEN//WIDOWS

Dewey Decimal Classification: 301.41
Library of Congress Catalog Card Number: 76-5298

Printed in the United States of America

Contents

	Prologue	7
1	Singular Female in a Paired Society	11
2	Myths, Miseries, and Ms.	22
3	The Many Faces of the Nonmarried Ms: Never-married Eve	37
4	The Many Faces of the Nonmarried Ms: The Formerly Married	51
5	Mother Without Father	63
6	Ten Commandments for a Solo Mother	77
7	Steward of My Body	88
8	Being Single *and* of Sound Mind	101
9	Freedom to Become	116
10	A Woman's Privilege: To Change Her Status	136
	Epilogue	160

Prologue

When is an idea-seed fertile enough to bring forth a book-child? There is no doubt that the germ of this book goes far back into the wholesomeness and pleasure of my young singleness. But it was watered and cultivated by some casual and not-so-casual "accidents" over the years. As when I read the best-seller by a certain bachelor career girl—a kind of how-to book for making it in the big city with only a good basic black dress and a "swinging" temperament. The thought flickered through my mind, later silently came back to lodge there dormant, "Surely, there is more to say about the full life to the millions of single women in this country than what the understated little black dress and the boss' bedroom say to the big city swingle."

Another nudge for writing this book was probably a student seminar I was asked to lead for a group of student nurses some ten years ago, "If I Don't Get Married, I'll Shoot Myself." That wacky title not only promoted some real inventory time on my part, it also provided the catalyst for one of the most provocative group sessions I've ever been a part of. I chuckled away the young nurses' suggestion that the time had come for a book written for serious singles!

This incident came up in the conversation several years

later as our single college professors gathered in my living room for one of our regular "specialty suppers." Soon we were all cataloging the questions we get asked about our singleness, the pet peeves we have, but also the host of rich experiences that have set us apart and given us the "second blessing."

It took several years of traveling here and there speaking to nonmarrieds before I determined to fill in some gaps in the growing blob of books for and about the never-marrieds and the formerly married. By the time I knew I was really committed to the task, I had ammasses hundreds of anonymous questionnaires from these, my people, about their joys, needs, and frustrations. So there are a lot of people walking through these few pages, most of whom do not even carry fictitious names. There are times when I believe some of them were the most devout, the saddest, the most beautiful, the most bitter, the most generous, the most alone—but I am sure it was only because they came very close for a very short time with very bare selves!

Some I have known spread across the years and into the fabric of my life: "Miss Malda," who was single during three periods of her life and developed an expertise in adjusting to each restructured life-style in a manner that was worthy of emulation. Miss Ivey, another octogenarian who was always and eternally single, reassured me that those who walk singly through life may understand more about and have greater capacity for love than many who are coupled.

There was M.A.T. whose chosen blueprint for her singleness was thwarted everywhere except in her soul, but she taught me that freedom is a gift of the spirit, and she kept it intact. Among many others, D.K.C. stands out because she loves with the devotion of a nun, gives with the largess of a millionairess, and enjoys with the openness of a trusting child.

Who could ask for anything more? But I do, when I ask that the singles and others who read this book do so with the same perspective with which I have written it. May you be confident, hopeful, and caring. Be assured that wholeness is a singular achievement, independent of your circumstance. It can happen to the unpaired in the midst of a broken world. I have seen it happen.

Sarah Frances Anders

1
Singular Female in a Paired Society

Growing up in America for today's median adults meant believing that almost all good things still come in pairs. If you were born before three wars in as many decades had upset the sex balance, you were probably conditioned also to think *matched* pairs—whether in socks, the original animals of Noah's ark, parents, restrooms, or Popsicles. Ours was a marrying tradition. To be perfectly accurate, it was a marrying *and* remarrying life-style, for our generation was so recently removed from the agrarian culture that reentering the marital state soon after widowhood was due more to habit than to economic necessity.

The quick changes wrought in the marital patterns of Americans in only two decades focused attention on two minority groups, now very visible and very vocal—the singles and the women. About a decade ago it suddenly seemed that a singles subculture had emerged overnight—manifested in Singles Tours, Swinging Singles Condominiums, computerized dating, and all kinds of singles organizations. Simultaneously in the 1960's a new self-consciousness was emerging among women—a new feminism was born. If you were a spectator on the American scene, you saw these two merge and begin to challenge the old images of the unmarried, weaker-of-the-two sexes! The single woman was *not* going to be accepted as the odd half of a broken pair of scissors as suggested by Ben Franklin. It seemed that she was not content to be an inconspicuous and second-class citizen in either a man's world or a couple's world.

This was the sentiment expressed in the prologue of the first issue of the short-lived *Single* magazine that appeared in the early 1970's:

How do single people find love, friendship, fulfillment? How do they cope with the problems? Why are so many choosing not to marry? Why are others seeking alternatives to marriage?

Single was created to serve the needs of this growing segment of society. We are not against marriage and we do not advocate any particular life-style, but we do reserve the right to fight both overt and subtle discrimination against singles.

For too long the single has been regarded as a second-class citizen. Throughout our magazine we intend to show that single adults can and should have the same rights, status, and self-esteem now enjoyed by the married. Only then will the single person be able to take his or her rightful place in society.

Careful reading of history, of course, can reveal those rare unmarried women of past centuries who rose above second-class citizenship imposed because of the pair of albatross they wore. Outstanding women such as Florence Nightingale, Joan of Arc, and Jane Addams would have distinguished themselves in any time or place, using their remarkable gifts for the social and intellectual advancement of mankind. There is a strong possibility that their places in history's hall of fame would have been diminished had they carried the additional responsibilities of husbands and many children. Today the possibility of economic independence and a greater freedom to choose marriage or singleness increases the likelihood of women pursuing social and personal betterment without benefit of a marriage partner.

The nonmarried woman today belongs to a myriad and growing species. This does not surprise you when you consider that men have not outnumbered women in our population since 1940. Those three war experiences in as many decades have combined with other factors to deplete the number of marriageable men and to prevent seven million women from having equal opportunity to the option of marriage. What is surprising is that the gap existing between the never-marrieds and the formerly marrieds is diminishing for women, but not for men.

The life-style of colonial America when over 95 percent of the women were married seems remote and alien. Singleness, for whatever reason, was a liability to a woman and to a farming society. If she were not physically or mentally handicapped, she still was only half productive as an individual and as a contributing member of a teamwork economy. Even if she rendered more than her fair share of individual production, she was not doing her part reproductively toward the future labor force of such an economy. Today, if you are a single woman you may be an asset to our society not only because you can be self-sufficient economically but also because you are not adding reproductively to an overpopulated environment where too many are already unemployed.

The Label "Single"

When does one *become* single? Is it a particular moment of self-awareness in a young woman's life or is it when society makes her self-conscious by attaching the label "single" to her—or both? Acknowledging that everyone is single for some post-puberty period, when is that point when others' perception of you stimulates self-perception (or vice versa) and you become socially aware of "being single"? For each person, it is a singular experience. For me, it first came at high school graduation. At sixteen, I was appalled that the *smartest* girl in our class, the valedictorian, was getting married and I was elated to be staying "single." Two years later, college degree and one lapsed engagement in hand, there was the somewhat smug new view of being a *chosen* single who would continue education and remain single for a *time*.

Many women authors and nonauthors have commented on the contrivance of our various publics to keep us aware of being single! During our early twenties it would be easier if we could avoid family reunions and old school friends for conscious and some not-so-conscious reasons. Loved ones as well as strangers seem to declare "open season" on singles, with an apparent abandonment of usual courtesy and tact. The two perennial questions that have brought me amusement over the years (and oftentimes prompted tart, impulsive retorts) were: "Are you *still* going to school?" (As if I were the only slow learner in our family!) and "Whatever happened to that last *nice* young fellow you were dating and we were so sure you were going to marry?" (This said all in one rushing breath, replete with subtle intonations, that there was surely something strange about my behavior and that I was beginning a pattern of always a bridesmaid . . .") As Sarah Jepson suggested in *For the Love of Singles*, few singles would say to their married friends, 'Why on earth *did you* get married?"

Even though there are specific moments of becoming legally widowed, whether by death or divorce, the formerly married sometimes have a time lag before their consciousness level reaches that moment of truth—"I'm *single* again." These once-marrieds often block out that period of being single in their premarriage days. Is it possible that adjustments (or lack of them) to living in a nonmarried state in later years to some extent reflect the earlier self-perception and adjustment in being single?

Her Social Profile

How do you draw a social portrait of 25 million nonmarried women in America? No more easily or accurately than you would for the 47 million (1975) who are married. Contemporary clichés about the nonmarried in our society just do not paint a full and true picture of them. "Swinging Spinsters," "sweet'n sour singles," "emancipated maidens," "Delilah Divorcee," "unclaimed blessings," "bachelor girl," "grass widow"—each denotes a stereotyped life-style label that would be damaging and misleading if applied to all singles. All that they suggest is that the nonmarried females in our population are a kaleidoscope of personalities and characteristics. They cut across all educational and age groups, social classes, religions, and occupations.

There are some patterns that emerge, however, as one takes an overview of the single, widowed, separated, and divorced women. Certainly even the casual observer can readily see that unmarried Americans are rapidly leaving minority status behind, although marriage and marrieds still dominate the value system of our culture. At least one third of all women over eighteen years of age are not living with a spouse and that makes them larger than any other "minority group"—blacks, Indians, unemployed, or senior citizens. This is the marital picture of American women:*

Marital Status	No. (in millions) Over 18 years	%
Married	46.2	65.6
Never-married	9.9	13.8
Separated	2.1	2.9
Widowed	9.6	13.4
Divorced	3.1	4.3
	70.9	100.0

*Current Population Reports, "Marital Status and Living Arrangements." Series P-20, No. 242, November 1972.

Although most American women will marry before they are twenty-one, 8 or 9 percent may never marry. Never-marrieds are the most numerous among the unattached women, but those who are widowed by death are a very close second. The formerly marrieds who have not remarried comprise 60 percent of all single women and about 20 percent of all women. It is significant that most women who are often stereotyped with such unique "single" life-styles have in fact been exposed to two family experiences—their parental families and their now-terminated marital families.

There is no indication that American women are making a sweeping move away from or against marriage. In fact, their dissolution and remarriage rate is noticeably higher than that of American males. In 1970, 22 percent of the men had been widowed, divorced, or both, but 34 percent of the women had had one or more marriages dissolved in either or both of these ways.

There is no dangerous age for becoming prone to singleness; no age group has the sole claim on a special type. However, you would expect certain kinds of singleness to predominate in particular age spans. Women who have never married tend to be in their twenties and early thirties. Separation is a threat to marriages of less than ten years duration particularly, so women are most vulnerable between twenty-five and thirty-five years of age. Divorcees are mainly in the median adult years, whereas widows abound in the over forty-five age group.

Ethnically, white women dominate the single scene only in numerical strength; 16 percent of all unattached women are non-Caucasian. Yet almost one half of the women in other racial groups are single (18.8 percent) or formerly married (28.2 percent). Separations are three times as likely to occur among blacks and other ethnic women.

Singles are a migratory group and nonmarried women particularly are urban-bound. Only widows are slower to pull up roots and head for the greener economic fields of metropolitan centers. Unmarried and divorced women flock to these population pockets not just to find the jobs which are more attractive and numerous there, but perhaps also to meet other singles. However, the sex ratio in the city becomes imbalanced and unfavorable as far as remarriage possibilities are concerned. Hence, the chances of remarriage would be even bleaker for all unmarrieds if many of the older rural widows were not content with their pension checks or social assistance.

Although most unattached women live in their own homes, some become secondary members of a relative's family. If a woman placed marriage in a priority spot above pure economic opportunity, she would head west toward Hawaii or north toward Alaska and North Dakota where unattached men abound. Instead, other factors appear to operate in keeping her in the metropolitan centers of the Northeast and Washington D.C. Certain states do attract particular types of women—older ones go to Florida, younger ones to California, divorcees to Nevada.

Single women could wield much more voting power over their male counterparts. Studies of recent election data and the voting behavior of the sexes indicates that interesting differences appear in choice of candidates and critical issues according to the sex of the voter. The seven million edge held by nonmarried women is largely an untapped source of power probably due to the fact that the two largest categories of these singles are the younger never marrieds (18-30 years) and the older widows who for quite different reasons are not exercising their full balloting strength.

The sixteen million women who are heads of households offer a challenge to the traditional concept of a patriarchal household. A great many of these are parents without partners or have the major support of one or both of their dependent elderly parents. Most of these women are not dependent on sources of support such as widow's pensions or alimony since singles make up about 30 percent of our labor force. The divorced and single are more apt to be in the labor force than the widowed. There is some indication that all kinds of single women are concentrated in selected occupations rather than randomly employed throughout the labor market. The single woman, almost as much as the bachelor, is being drawn toward traveling positions and those with erratic hours that are hard on family life. In the past, the ministry, government positions, and executive posts were biased against the unmarried person, particularly the female, but there are indications that this type of discrimination is diminishing.

There is clear evidence then that nonmarrieds suffer some economic disadvantages in our society. We will discuss this again in later chapters. Those with no dependents pay disproportionately high property and income taxes (up to $500 more per year in moderate income brackets). Those who are widowed and divorced may enter the labor market late in life and, though they may be well-educated, lack the seniority and tenure that would assure them income comparable to their peers. This is reflected in the fact that women heads of households earn about $4,000 less than male heads, but earn at least $7,000 less than complete families. The never-married fare better salary-wise both because of their extra years of schooling and longer tenure in the work force. One of the most interesting differences appears between men and women who are never married careerists. By middle age, women often have significantly more education and consequently higher professional status. This is the one marital group in which women exceed men in their median annual incomes.

Minority or Minerva?

I have already suggested that perhaps neither singles nor women (nor single women) entirely justify the label of minority or subculture. True, in a society that still vouchsafes marriage and the conjugal home through almost 47 million intact married couples, the 25 million unattached women among almost 42 million total singles over 18 years of age appears to be a rapidly growing, but still a statistical minority. Yet the concept *minority* among behavioral scientists implies status and treatment as much as numbers. Is there support for the belief that single women have been relegated to inferior status, abused, forgotten, or thwarted in the same manner that history records for blacks, Indians, Mexican-Americans, or Orientals?

Over recent years I have questioned over 500 nonmarried women across our nation, in both religious and secular conferences. They cut across all ages, almost evenly divided among the under forty and over forty. They have responded very candidly about their roles and treatment in society. The majority (60 percent) felt that there are still more disadvantages than advantages to being unmarried.

With equal honesty and little indication of paranoia, 85 percent of these women indicated that they at times felt like "fifth wheels" in social situations, but only one fourth said this was a frequent feeling. Nearly all of them believed that society put some stigma on singleness, but less than half of them felt that it had any appreciable influence on their moods or personality. More than half of them, however, indicated that being single was something of an asset in their jobs and that their church made little or no difference in its treatment of them as members.

Understandably, their greatest frustrations came in the entertainment and financial areas of their lives. It is still more difficult for any unmarried woman to attend many public entertainment places unescorted. Because these women were predominately under forty and in the low-to-moderate income levels ($5,000—12,000), they could be expected to experience some problems with their budgets.

What I have concluded is that most single women are conscious of lower status when it comes to concrete symbols such as income and job titles, but there is little obsessive concern with mistreatment or rejection on the part of church and society. Some critics would say these women have been brainwashed, that they rationalize away too many disadvantages. But it would be difficult to believe that this would be true with respect to the 13 percent of these single women who were in upper white-collar, managerial, and executive positions. Many of them see it as a "fact of life" that society is paired. It also seems reasonable that those who have shared the paired existence for a time would feel more acutely the experience of being a "fifth wheel" when unattached.

To suggest that singles represent a rapidly growing homogeneous subculture that may be a threat to the dominant American family pattern is equally erroneous. There appears to be as much divergence among the lifestyles of nonmarried women and men as we know exists among married persons. The ideal nuclear family of a two-generation household, with parents and unmarried children, has historically probably been just that—ideal. That single women life-styles are multivariant is the thesis of this book and will be discussed more fully in chapter 3.

There seem to be similarities between today's nonmarried woman and Minerva of mythology. This goddess was never married and was called the Maiden. She was the favored child of her father Zeus and multitalented. She could be fierce and embattled when home and country were threatened; she could be creative in arts and crafts or inventive when need arose. Athens was her urbane residence, the olive tree her productive symbol, and the owl her symbol of wisdom. If the never-marrieds and formerly marrieds are not the favored children of society now, there still may be some prophetic tones to this analogy. If you are a modern Minerva, you are productive without being overly reproductive and you are underpaid while carrying a better than average tax load to help provide for needier segments of our population. You are part of a sisterhood, busy in many helping vocations and serving in countless civic and church volunteer programs that make society more livable.

Some Related Readings

Andrews, Gini. *Your Half of the Apple*. Family Concern, Inc., Box 4249, Omaha, Nebraska; or Zondervan Press.

Mumaw, Evelyn K. *Woman Alone*. Herald Press, 1970.

Narramore, Clyde M. *The Unmarried Woman*. Zondervan, 1961.

Narramore, Clyde M. *A Woman's World*. Chapter 3 Zondervan, 1963.

O'Brien, Patricia. *The Woman Alone*. Quadrangle, 1974.

Payne, Dorothy. *Women Without Men*. United Church, 1969.

Seskin, Jane. *Living Single*. Price Stern, 1974.

Smith, Blanche M. *The Single Woman of Today*. Greenwood (1951, 1974).

Taves, Isabella. *Women Alone*. Funk and Wagnalls, 1969.

2
Myths, Miseries, and Ms.

A single professional woman friend of mine recently spoke in mock exasperation, "I wish the New Testament writers hadn't been so silent on the social tactics used by the strong 'single' characters who parade through the biblical pages! When you consider Jesus and Paul, for instance, even as religious celibates they were not typical for their times. There must have been overwhelming pressure on them from Jewish tradition and social mythology about bachelors—how did they cope?"

I confessed that I had not given much thought until then to the number and kinds of nonmarrieds in the Bible. Of course, some scholars have contended that Paul was married. But she was right—who laughed when Jesus and Paul, apparently lifelong bachelors, spoke strongly and eloquently of love, marital problems, questions of family relationships and spiritual loyalty, children, and a host of other social issues that unmarrieds aren't supposed to know about? How did they overcome the myth that experience is the only reliable teacher when it comes to marriage, sex, or family problems?

I realized that probably some of the disciples were not married. I discovered that the "parade of unattached women" began to grow as I contemplated biblical characters to whom I had never assigned marital status. Who whispered about the visit of Jesus to the home of the "maiden ladies," Mary and Martha? Martha may have been a widow and head of the household simply by virtue of the fact that she at one time *was* married and was now devoid of romantic, youthful thoughts. Mary certainly was not creaking with mental or physical arthritis and age if she could sit on the floor at Jesus' feet and talk about "men's" deeper topics of conversations! Were there constant suspicions to deal with concerning the widows and wives who probably followed along to support and serve the needs of the disciples? Did Jesus have to suffer comments about "momism" when his mother showed up with his brothers to persuade him to come home?

Did Paul encounter myths about the role of single women in the freer Greek community? Is this why he cautioned all of the Christian women to maintain quiet decorum in and out of church lest they be mistaken for the aggressive and pagan Greek women of the world, the hetaera? Did Lydia, the well-to-do businesswoman, encounter much prejudice as she managed a successful and expensive fabric outlet in a man's world? Was she considered out of line with her feminine role when she, Euodias, and Syntyche labored alongside Paul in evangelism and used her comfortable home for the Philippian church? Did Paul receive any backlash from his commendation of Phebe as she journeyed to Rome and greeted the Christian friends there virtually as his emissary?

Admittedly, every age and culture has maintained role systems based on sex, age, and marital status. Even when a society has distinguished behavioral patterns where the sexual roles are interchangeable without a rigid ranking system, the destiny and necessity of marriage have permitted very few single roles with preferred status. Two to four centuries ago there were religious celibates, temple virgins, ascetics, and eunuchs in many parts of the world. The cultures of the Hebrews, Romans, and Greeks provided highly stylized roles for single women. For a woman to remain unmarried without being dedicated to one of these acceptable roles as temple virgin, hetaera, or church widow was to invite wrath, stigmata, or exile from society.

The situation we find in the United States today is a highly fluid, even unstable system of roles. During the last twenty years many Americans have genuinely feared that the inevitable changes produced by an upsurge in the unmarried and female populations were related to the unisexual trends among young and old in dress, hairstyles, and interests. Even many single women who, of necessity, moved into predominantly male economic areas protested their desire to remain "feminine." So, contemporary single women must deal with the cultural lag of a double mythology carried over from the nineteenth century: What is acceptable behavior for a single person *and* a woman? Let's look at some of the recurring myths which single and formerly married women reported that they have encountered. They can readily be discussed under biological, psychological, social, and religious fallacies.

Biological Myths

Myth I. *The only normal and happy life-style for a woman is that shared with a mate.* Countless numbers of women have reported their resentment that a woman is assumed to be inherently more dependent than a man on having a mate and the security of a marriage. While Freud certainly didn't invent this notion, his theory that "anatomy is destiny" has had a damning and dampening effect on the acceptance of women as "single families." He moved from the disturbing envy of the girl because she was not born a boy to the "mature" adult phase where she accepts her inferior sex status and the next best role in life—being the lifelong associate and complement to the superior mate. This forces any person, male or female, into the absurd and non-Christian position of placing biological completeness in heterosexual union as the ultimate priority of life.

A preacher friend of mine, usually insightful and tolerant, made an appalling assertion in a public meeting. He said that every woman who was honest with herself would have to admit that the ultimate aim of *every* woman was to be married to the right man. He further said that the ultimate frustration was for a woman to end her life without ever having been married. I could only assume that there was no comparable aim or frustration in a male's experience that remotely approached this feminine deprivation.

Can a society that bases its values on lifelong monogamous relations, but has a decided imbalance in the sex ratio of its adult population, afford such a myth? Hardly, when it deplores, with Christian pronouncements, any violation of marital sanctity or legal dissolution of the relationship.

Christians who believe in the creation of equal worth in all persons, regardless of sex, race, or culture, find it difficult to buy Lionel Tiger's "bonding theory" of male relationships. Can you accept the notion that women have never been capable of a David and Jonathan relationship, that all women reject the bonding experience with others of their own sex because they are innately suspicious, uncomfortable, and jealous of them? Is it necessarily logical or believable to the Christian woman that cultures have been right or true to the biological natures of both sexes in permitting the males to go in hunting groups, to form all-male fraternal orders, to establish sometimes warmer and more intimate relationships with a male comrade than with a spouse, yet not consider it proper for women to seek the same social relationships?

The viable Christian position would seem to be rather that there are a number of acceptable life-styles which the mature Christian will find normal and happy. Being married is no more an insurance policy for happiness than singleness is guaranteed frustration and unhappiness. Happiness is not biologically determined. Numerous studies indicate that the happiest married persons were those who had not rushed into marriage to escape unhappy homes or loneliness as singles, but had first established a sense of well-being and happiness in being single.

Myth II. *The natural and major fulfillment of a woman is to be a mother*. This is the logical extension of the assumption that the basic law of a female's life is to mate; heterosexual mating must be fulfilled in procreation of new life. Dr. Benjamin Spock picked up with the aftermath of Freudian theories about the relationship of the sexes and the crucial parent-child relationship in infancy. The optimum craft of any woman, Spock declared, is the bearing and the molding of a child, in a very special mold, to be sure. "Behind every great man is a great woman—his mother" and "the hand that rocks the cradle rules the world" are axioms which reinforced the notion that a woman might be crucial in the shaping of a *young* child, but men and male institutions had best take over after puberty! It also suggested that the major claim to renown open to a woman was through the careful molding of a male child who would make a better world. He was her link to a meaningful future.

A part of the salve (which made single and married women assume that mating and motherhood were their ordained sources of total fulfillment) was the implication that women were better at these roles. Not just because they had the ovaries, uterus, and breasts for bearing and nurture—but because they were innately more sensitive, religious, and morally perceptive. Here were the bedrocks of future generations which an unmarried woman obviously could not share in. But this notion was equally demeaning to the nature and potential of the male, married or single.

One might be misled to believe that any nonmarried

woman who is one of the almost half-million who are having children out of wedlock is destined to be more fulfilled personally and more profitable to society! Equally disturbing is the notion that the childless married woman is more of a threat to the native role of womankind than the unwed or divorced mother. While Jesus used some biological analogies as he spoke of hungering and thirsting after righteousness, he never intimated that mating and reproduction were the criteria for entering the kingdom of heaven. He did explicitly suggest that married and single alike must be "born again" in a totally nonbiological process!

Myth III. *The single woman is usually biologically abnormal and/or unattractive.* Most of the single, separated, and divorced women who commented on this myth did so in apparent good humor. But underneath the bemusement rankled a touch of disgust since it is readily apparent that all married persons are neither biologically sound nor beautiful people! Indeed, only a bit of research is necessary to see that the biologically inferior are drawn like magnets to each other in marriage—the handicapped in sight, hearing, or movement, as well as in size, weight, and looks. There is also perennial amazement at the opposites who attract in physical appearance and health.

If anything, the unmarried and formerly married women give more attention to their appearances than many married persons. With cosmetic and health transformations that are equally marketable to married and single, it hardly seems necessary for anyone to be totally unattractive in this age.

Psychological Myths

Myth IV. *Due to abnormal childhoods, nonmarried women are antimen, antifamily, antichildren, even antifeminine.* What a blanket misstatement this is! Only recently I heard two quite different women, one a Vietnam widow with two small children and one a career single in a top-ranking corporation position, make the same observation about themselves, "I think I really prefer the company of men. Actually some of my best friends are my male associates and not just because I work with them. I doubt if I ever could be content to talk 'typical' female talk even if I never worked out again—I just have broader interests than most of my homemaker friends. I love children, but I don't want to talk diapers, dishes, and diseases all the time." Even if these statements show some overgeneralizations about homemakers, the trend of thought is still important.

The greatest tragedy of women's behavior in our time may go down in history not as the number of women who did not endorse family life and motherhood, for most studies indicate that even radical feminists may not differ from most women on this issue. It is that so many women have had children who never should have been mothers. Somehow we all must agree that the several million women who never marry and have children but who devote themselves to teaching, social work, nursing others' children seem more psychologically sound than the millions who consistently abuse and neglect their children. A recent Health, Education, and Welfare Department report says that 1.5 to 2 million cases of child abuse will be reported annually and that one fifth of these infants will die from such treatment or neglect. Another probable thousand or so children's deaths will occur as "accidents" due to the neglect of parents. These parents-that-should-never-have-been cut across all kinds of communities and classes of people; they are psychologically in worse shape than most nonmarrieds we know.

Myth V. *Due to their erratic and emotional behavior, single women do not make reliable employees.* Jessie Bernard's study of mental health and marital status refutes this notion. Single women were emotionally more stable than either bachelors or married women. Because they also tended to have more schooling than the bachelors, there was a higher percentage of them in professional and managerial positions, and they were making appreciably more in salary. Of course, a contributing factor to the latter situation is the fact that some men have tended to bypass the well-trained and successful women as possible mates, preferring to down-marry in education and status.

There is no indication that nonmarried women miss work more than men, although married women average about two days more a year in disability than men, probably due to pregnancy and childbearing absenteeism. Bachelors and unmarried women spend more days in the hospital when they go, largely due to the fact that there is no one at home to care for them. If the formerly married appear to have poorer health, have more neuroses, commit more criminal offenses, and die younger, we can't assume that they are a biologically and psychologically inferior group. It may be that their life-style and marital problems have been determinants in these disorders and not vice versa. Family life is generally healthier for people; but if one is mentally or physically disabled, he is less likely to disturb and infect the lives of others if he is not married!

My own study of working singles indicates that they are more flexible when there is need for extra duties or longer working hours. They also are generally less complaining than family persons in these same job demands.

Myth VI. Another false assumption about nonmarried women is that *their psychological umbilical cords have not been cut with the parental family*. There is some confusion here between concern for parents and independence from them. It is true that women, married or single, have been more responsive to the needs of aging parents whether or not they express it by moving them into their own households. Yet nonmarried women are more likely to live independently from their parents, even heads of their households, than are nonmarried men. This is true whether they are single, widowed, or divorced.

When a friend of mine was questioned about how her mother had made the adjustments necessary as she sold her properties and moved nearby her single daughter, she laughingly replied, "Oh, she has adjusted wonderfully well. Who would ever thought that a sweet little octogenarian, twice-widowed with fifty-year-old roots in her church and community, could have acclimated and accommodated herself so rapidly to a new environment? I'm the one who's still getting used to the idea! After being away from home and mostly in other states for over 25 years, living an independent life-style, I'm having difficulty shifting gears, and it has nothing to do with not accepting the idea nor wanting to adjust!"

Myth VII. *Unmarried women are frustrated sexually and more apt to engage in deviant behaviors.* In reply to a confidential questionnaire dealing in part with problem areas and frustrations of being single, the area of sex ranked third or fourth in order of concern. Generally concerns about acceptable entertainment, finances, rewarding friendships, and children take precedence over sexual frustrations. There seems to be about the same distribution of "hypererotics," moderates, and frigid women among the married as among the nonmarried. There is no absolute evidence that singles even abound among prostitutes! We do not have studies on homosexuals among married women comparable with those of men, but from the evidence on male homosexuality, we might assume that marriage has often been a cloak for many Lesbian women, too.

When one considers the somewhat invisible but strongly suspected promiscuity among married persons in occasional adultery, wife-swapping, and the like as compared to the more visible deviances among some nonmarrieds, it could be similar to comparing a tip of the crime iceberg—youthful first-offenders with the massive, less visible, and more expensive crimes of white-collar professionals and corporations. It may be minimal in comparison.

One of the most interesting things I have unearthed among nonmarrieds is that more than half readily admitted to feeling some frustration sexually, but felt that, to some extent, being restricted sexually had tended to make them more creative in other areas. Sublimation was, to them, not necessarily a cramping and nonproductive experience. Very few felt a great deal of sexual frustration, but three fourths of these women believed that the church and society should be no more permissive in sexual standards for the unmarried than for the married. Once again, my counseling with marrieds indicates that marriage does not preclude sexual frustrations!

Social Myths

Myth VIII. *The traditional roles are still the most comfortable for women.* Of course, in previous centuries these feminine roles were hardly distinguishable, whether one was married or not. The only distinctions in a woman's behavior depended on her class status, whether she was of the hardy, earthy peasant stock or the genteel, pampered nobility. If she were a have-not, she worked alongside her menfolk with the stock and in the fields, taking little time out when she birthed, cooked, and tended the house. If she, by accident of birth, belonged to the elite class, she was considered frail, placed on a pedestal, or considered frivolous in most cultures. She was in many ways the forerunner of the *Playboy* bunny, in that she was a delightful toy to spend leisure time with but not to be included in the deeper discussions and problems of life.

The four areas of the classical German woman's life were typical of earlier cultures—*kinder* (children), *kuche* (kitchen), *kirche* (church) and *kleiden* (clothing). If a female were widowed, orphaned, or single, she might venture out of her father's house to become a nursemaid or governess (*kinder*), a domestic (*kleiden* or *kuche*), or a nun (*kirche*). Later, her nursing, seamstress, waitress, and teaching roles would simply be extensions of the acceptable female roles in the home.

Twentieth-century women who are not currently married and perforce are in the labor market still concentrate in those occupations which are extensions of the traditional roles: teaching in the lower grades, nursing, social work, clerks in ready-to-wear, secretaries who make coffee and generally housekeep at the office. For the woman head of a household, this may often seem like doing "double-duty" in the domestic chores. Yet it is a role that they have seemed to willingly accept until recent years. Seeing nonmarried women make it in law, medicine, government, college teaching, engineering, and other previously male jobs has struck a corresponding chord among married women. Indeed, sometimes it has been the other way around!

Myth IX. *The hormonal patterns of a woman and the frustrations of being single combine to make her unpredictable in critical decision-making positions.* One prominent doctor stated publicly several years ago that we could never have a woman president—because the crucial time for her to pick up the red "emergency" phone in international affairs might come at the low point in her menstrual cycle, and she could not be expected to make a reliable decision. Oh, the wrath of his own wife's response the next day! It is true that studies have shown some women may be more accident-prone or tense just before and during the menstrual period, but this is not to say that it is the *universal* case for all women, or that single women experience more or less tension and moodiness at these times. What is more revealing is that a recent group of studies indicates a definite *male* cycle which does appear to correlate with mood and behavioral changes!

Myth X. Many are led to believe that *single people in general are a drain on society*; that if they are going to mental and medical hospitals more, committing more crimes, and are generally "different," then they are costing society more in services than married people. The answer is almost too obvious. Nonmarrieds pay more taxes (and tithes) per capita with less salaries. Many of them are in the helping professions themselves and appear to be alleviating some ills in society. Some are working with other people's problem children. Yet often the agencies of social service are oriented toward family needs, not single problems. A widow's benefits seldom compare to her husband's retirement income, and there are more divorcees who are self-supporting because of fewer legal decisions in their favor on alimony or child support.

Myth XI. *Single women need help in finding a mate.* Having worked as a single career woman in two professions in five different states, I know that matchmakers are a universal species with wonderfully genuine and caring motives. Again, some of my best friends have been matchmakers! Many nonmarrieds have maintained that far worse than being the "fifth wheel" at a social affair is being paired with the "perfect" eligible male. You wonder how you can have been such close friends with these matchmakers for so long a time and they understand you so little!

Add to this a strong suspicion that many unattached women would prefer some male already broken in and you can have instant tension in even an old friendship between married and nonmarried women. It may well be that an unattached woman feels more comfortable with a married male friend who won't necessarily think she is using her feminine wiles on him and whose wife she trusts will understand that she regards them as an inseparable pair of friends. Unfortunately, the same woman who points out the shortcomings in her mate rather critically and occasionally prods him to change may assume that he looks like an ideal male to a woman friend who has had a bitter failure in marriage or recently been bereft in the loss of her beloved husband.

Religious Myths

Myth XII. There is the suggestion as one reads history that in the more devoutly religious (even Protestant!) civilizations, *a woman was regarded as not as blessed of the Lord if she were not married and fruitful*. This no doubt stems from ancient writings which indicates that if daughters married out of order, the younger married one would be casting aspersions on the normalcy of the older sister, as in the case of Leah and Rachel in the story of Jacob. It was also manifest in the self-perception of Sarah when she assumed she was not in full favor with God since he left her barren throughout her childbearing cycle.

The early New Testament church did provide unique positions for the nonmarried women of the fellowship. Biblical scholars point out that young maidens (virgins) were used in the service of the church until such time as marriage and childbearing released them from this special commitment to the church. There were the servants (ministers) such as Phebe (who I believe was a deacon) who served alongside the men in carrying out the witnessing and ministry of the church. There seemed to be no distinctions in tasks by marital status or sex. There were also the widows who received support from the church as they tended to the ill, the orphans, and needy of the community. In the first few centuries of the church, women, both married and single, assisted in administering the ordinances to the believers.

During the Dark Ages, single women escaped the inflexible domestic role by taking church vows. The conventual life sometimes provided the only art, music, and literacy available to a woman. Even widows often entered convents later in life and some founded special healing and teaching orders.

Contemporary unmarried women, like married ones, have often chafed under the restrictive church roles open to them. When they hold professional church positions, it is usually in the areas of music and children's work, and the assumption is that marriage will remove them from the "call." Although women dominate the church membership numerically, as they do the general population, single ones do not have equal access to major committees and decision-making, either with the men or with their married sisters. An interesting contrast is the trend toward women missionaries, not solely married ones sent as helpmeets, but even single and widowed ones during the past 100 years.

The Magical Ms.

One of the most ambivalent issues in recent feminism, among the married and nonmarried, is the acceptance of the nondistinguishing title for all women, Ms. It has created as much confusion perhaps as it has prevented. Certainly, it shows little magical power for erasing mythology about single women! The greatest boon has probably been to the addresser, not to the postal service and certainly not to all the addressees.

Theoretically, society has no doubt needed an equalizing term for women comparable to Mister (Mr.) for all men. I confess there have been times when some of the strain of beginning relationships had me wishing that we had some "Americanese" for addressing bachelors, widowers, divorces, and husbands separately and distinctively! It is unclear at this moment in time if Ms. will aid in the search for the nonmarried woman's identity or if it will further obscure her role in our society. Hopefully, the confusion will be no greater than that experienced when a Southerner, in typical slurring says "Miz" for Mrs. and I don't know whether or not to correct him. Let us hope that Ms. doesn't create additional miseries!

This chapter has not intended to suggest that all of the difficulties single women face in our society today are due to lingering sexual mythology or titles. We will discuss many other sources of both frustration and satisfaction in the following chapters.

Some Suggested Books

Bernard, Jessie. *The Future of Marriage*. Bantam Books, 1972.
Colin, Jean. *Never Had It So Good*. Verry, 1974.
Greer, R. *Why Isn't a Nice Girl Like You Married?* Macmillan, 1969.
Thornton, Alice B. *How Come You're Not Married?* Chris Mass, 1966.

3
The Many Faces of the Nonmarried Ms: Never-married Eve

Virginia was born to be free and since she was born into a comfortably well-to-do family that would provide stock dividends for a reasonably carefree life, she looked forward to travel and adventure and the good, single life. After a prolonged college career of being a "favorite," a "beauty," and the recipient of a number of wonderful opportunities to marry, she graduated with expectancy for a responsible freedom. By thirty, however, she was settled into the household with her seventy-year-old parents and by forty she had the care of a niece's very young children, one as bright as the other was slow. She became a remarkable example of one who balances the responsibilities of dependents four generations apart for over twenty years. Yet she has never lost the spirit of travel, adventure, and freedom when the fates have seemed to plot against her.

* * *

Jackie was committed to foreign missions when I first knew her as a college student, and I watched this bright young student leader as she later entered social services in a children's home. A marriage to a preacher-student who was immature and disturbed after military service finally disintegrated in inevitable bitterness and disillusionment because of thwarted life plans. Now as an esteemed college professor and authoress, she has come through personal and family traumas that would have flattened less stalwart persons. She demonstrates the hard-won inner satisfaction of a replaced life goal which may have provided her an arena where she will touch far more lives than she would have on a mission field.

* * *

Marian reared her only son alone after the husband of her late teens disappeared into the horizon with another woman. She worked hard to be a strong mother for her now-married son, went to college at night, advanced in her work, and matured into a charming and poised forty-year-old. Active in church and still busy with advanced professional courses, she is independent of her son's young family. Propositioned by a variety of male types through her business contacts, she faces special adjustments to aloneness in the midst of busyness.

* * *

Sue-lynn came home following her father's death to be with her mother in her declining years and forced retirement. Forced to locate in less satisfying positions in paramedicine, she made her contentment through church associations, friends, nieces, and nephews. At forty, following her mother's death, she served for three years in two European hospitals. While abroad, she studied in Bible conferences on the side and traveled in all directions on holidays. Even now, she searches for another unusual niche back in the States where she can express her talents in humanitarian ways unhampered by systems and myths, free to explore many new kinds of relationships.

* * *

Deborah married right out of high school although she

had several college scholarship offers. Childless after the loss of an infant, she held a marriage together for over two decades, suffering an immature husband's infidelity, alcoholism, and ineptness. Finally taking the step of a legal separation, she tries to juggle the pieces of her life between a deep-seated fundamental religion that condemns divorce and that special brand of loneliness when one seems to have been married all of one's life. Holding down two jobs, going to school on weekends, yearning for compatible friends, she continues to grope for a new life-style as a bright median adult when very few available activities seem to challenge her unusual capabilities.

* * *

Cheryl, recent young missionary appointee to an African nation, wrote in The Commission *about the adjustments of a single woman in the midst of a culture where the only single women are prostitutes. Assumed to be inexperienced because of her singleness, she must work doubly hard to be accepted in the social service ministry she is dedicated to. Other missionary couples are occupied with their families; suitable bachelors are almost nonexistent; little household dilemmas become crises in a male-oriented society. Yet in her words, "I manage. And very well . . . it is just plain fascinating that God should love me enough to give his single girls a special sense of his presence . . . I wouldn't trade my single life in his service for anything."*

A highly selective and distorted collection of vignettes about the life-styles of nonmarried women in America? Not at all. These half-dozen women depict neither typical patterns nor the full measure of variability among the almost twenty-five million women who are not married.

Susan Jacoby wrote in the *New York Times Magazine* in 1974, "The diversity of single life . . . contradicts both the old-fashioned image of unmarried people as lonely losers and the current media picture of 'swingles' who cavort through an endless round of bars, parties and no-strings-attached sexual adventures." The reasons for women being unpaired and their subsequent life-styles are at least as numerous and varied as those given by their married peers for getting and staying married. There is no reason to assume that their pressures and rewards do not also match those of their married friends, in number if not in kind. Although there may be similarities of life-style that cut across the various types of nonmarriage, let's first take a look at those women who have never married.

Singleness as an Option

Most of the futurologists who discuss marriage in the coming generation remark on the expected upward trend in delaying or foregoing marriage. On one of the New Year's programs of the *Today* show in 1976, Barbara Walters asked a group of college and graduate students about their future marital plans. They were about evenly divided among those who planned to stay single (at least for a good while), those who expected at some time to cohabit with someone of the same or opposite sex, and those who planned a traditional marriage. While these men and women are hardly suggested as a representative group of young Americans, their responses do indicate that singleness is passing from an involuntary, pitiable circumstance to possibly an enviable, intentional option for many.

Very little scholarly research has been done until recently on the never-marrieds, either men or women. As a professor in marriage and family courses for two decades, I have been disturbed to find that only two or three of the better textbooks have dealt with the option of singleness and then only in a perfunctory way as if these individuals were by definition "deviant" in such a textbook. However, a 1975 special issue of *The Family Coordinator* had more than one author suggesting that singleness is emerging as both a rightful and voluntary option for today's youth.

In the late 1960's Paul Glick, a renowned marriage statistician, predicted that among the youth of that decade only about 3 or 4 percent would not eventually marry. But a dramatic trend began to appear in the seventies, indicated by 50 percent more singles between the ages of twenty and thirty-four years. Other studies have shown that young college women particularly shifted in their attitudes about marriage for themselves between their freshmen and senior years. A rather startling 40 percent of the senior girls in one eastern school were reported as not being certain that they would ever marry. Various college studies have suggested that this pattern is more than selective sampling or "trendy" girls. It reflects strong misgivings about marriage in general. Sociologist Peter Stein has indicated that 25 to 39 percent of the young women he questioned believed that traditional marriage was obsolete or that it would no longer work for our society. They either did not look forward to marriage or were uncertain that it would work for them. Perhaps his sample represented a more urban, secular, and nontraditional campus environment than would be true for all American young women, even college women. My own contacts with, and studies of, women in their late teens and twenties would not suggest overall disillusionment with the institution of marriage, even if they personally want to delay it for a time or permanently.

Among the nonmarrieds, single women are outnumbered by almost three million bachelors. However, they still hold a plurality among unattached women, but a bare edge over the widows who may be expected in another decade to exceed them. The option to stay single does not appear alarming or threatening to marriage at all when one considers that the formerly marrieds are more than 50 percent greater in number than the never-marrieds. Nevertheless, almost ten million single women are an intriguing and significant subpopulation, seeking new roles and acceptance in today's world.

Why *Versus* Why Not

Perhaps neither divorce nor widowhood piques the curiosity of the married population so much as the "whys" of singleness! Bishop Fulton Sheen on occasion has remarked that he liked to think of all the lovely young ladies he had helped make happy for a lifetime because he did not marry! Even though marriage is considered a personal decision, his response would not satisfy some people and sometimes even the unmarried are not sure of all their particular "homogenized" reasons for not being married.

We certainly seem far removed from the 1950's when Manfred Kuhn implied in one of the marriage and family texts that most singles were personal failures or they probably would have been married. According to him, most of the reasons for nonmarriage included hostility toward the institution of marriage or the opposite sex, homosexuality, a fixation on one's parents, unattractiveness, an unwillingness to accept responsibility, or simply not ever finding that idealized "right one" somewhere in this vast world. Consequently, a certain social inadequacy emerged and the single person inevitably became a misfit or social failure. There is no desire here to oversimplify or distort his conclusions, but most contemporary counselors would refute these as major reasons for singleness two decades later. Indeed, as one reviews the list, one must acknowledge that not a one of these factors is missing among the married!

Just as people marry for a variety of reasons—including the desire for children, the domestic life, a legitimate sex life, religious expectations, and security—the reasons for remaining single are legion and diverse. Seldom is it purely a matter of lack of opportunity, of being "passed by." All one need do is look around and observe that almost *any*body can *get* married. Being happily married and staying married are quite different matters. It is true that a considerable number of people today grow up in unhappy or broken families, but we can't assume that all of them turn against marriage or believe that they wouldn't do better with it than their parents did. Surely not all of the intact marriages of our grandparents and great-grandparents were ideal and happy, leaving a positive outlook on marriage or the opposite sex for all of the offspring.

A negligible proportion of women today do not marry because they have serious physical disabilities or severe emotional hangups. In fact, authorities on the family have suggested that single women are a superior breed to bachelors in this respect. Jessie Bernard has found in her studies that unmarried women are "spectacularly better off so far as psychological distress symptoms are concerned, suggesting that women start out with an initial advantage which marriage reverses." Bernard is only one among several researchers who have found that twice as many single men show mental health impairments. This is true at all age levels, but as single women grow older their mental health increasingly surpasses that of bachelors. Women show less distress in "being single" and are more active in working out their problems. They are generally far less likely to suffer from depression or antisocial tendencies.

What really puzzled Bernard was that single women fared so much better emotionally than did married ones. She talks about the "dwindling into marriage" process which appears to take place for many women who absorb themselves into their husband's life-styles but later appear to revolt against the Pygmalion drives of the male or society to cast her in his life-mold. Another obvious explanation of the poorer showing of married women in emotional well-being is the "chicken-and-egg" dilemma. Is the overall mental picture of married women affected by the particular type of emotionally immature girl who rushes into the "security" of marriage? Or to mix metaphors, does the inferior single woman jump from the frying pan into the fire? We have long known that the girl who rushes into early marriage appears less mature, poised, and socially secure than the girl who marries in her middle-to-late twenties or not at all.

Don't be misled by any of the earlier writers who suggested that single women liked to flaunt their economic independence, but in reality would never be able to compete favorably with men in the work world. These days, whatever discrepancies appear in the economic situation of women (married or single), it is not due to the inferiority of the species by gender or marital status, but rather it is usually the lingering discrimination from a male-dominated work world. Education, occupation, and salary all indicate that there is relative superiority of single women over single men. At any age, the single women have more training, more prestige, and higher income; but by middle age, the difference between them and bachelors is of canyon proportions. Overall, the single career woman has at least three years more schooling than the bachelor. Over 26 percent of them will achieve professional positions as compared with only 10 percent of the bachelors. It follows that the professional female will be able to demand and expect larger salary benefits.

Realizing that through Providence and genetics at least 50 percent of human aptitudes must surely be entrusted to women and that there are certain talents allegedly peculiar to them, the increasing opportunities to enter a wide range of vocations once closed to them provide satisfaction for many bright women. It is significant that among the twelve Women of the Year on the cover of the first 1976 issue of

Time were three single women; an author, a Congresswoman, and a State Supreme Court Justice. Ambition to be successful and to contribute to humanity through law, medicine, the arts, religion, politics, and science without being cumbered with a family does not have to indicate that a woman is selfish and egocentric. I will grant you that an absorbing position for some women may simply be an escape from past experiences with negative family life or romance and fear of future disappointment. For others work may be rewarding, fulfilling, and completely altruistic. It would be just as feasible to assume some married women use their jobs or careers to escape the housewife-mother syndrome of boredom or trivia. The fact that many successful women have combined family and professional options need not indicate that those who do not are abnormal or misfits.

For some young women, other responsibilities and opportunities take precedence over marriage. Often what seems at the outset only a reason for temporary postponement of marriage may persist until the pattern of a single life-style pretty much precludes late marriage. Unmarried daughters, more often than married children or bachelor sons, find it their lot to assume care for, and often even financial support of, aging parents. What may be a joy in many ways can also become a source of frustration as the natural desires to date and to socialize freely are inhibited. There is much need for a young woman caught in such circumstances (be it ever so willingly) to recognize her frustrations in leading a normal social life, rather than risk the possibilities of various psychosomatic illnesses resulting from repression.

The unmarried female, probably more than the widow or divorcee, faces the recurring biological myths, not only handed down from centuries of female domesticity but also reinforced by twentieth-century writers such as Freud and

Spock. As already discussed, the former confirmed the age-old notion that women were best suited for marriage and household duties because they were biologically weaker and emotionally more erratic. They were obviously structurally designed to be incubators and psychologically blueprinted for nurturing the young. Spock later suggested that woman was best at molding children, but there is the subtle implication that even here she needs the long-term design drawn by the male and she mainly provides the shaping in the tender years. Even the church has supported this in much of its literature when it portrays only the cultural roles of women in the Hebrew, early Christian and agrarian societies. From children's departments up, the stories and lessons in church school have stressed the importance of the maternal and nurturing roles of women to the neglect or exclusion of her sharing business and other nondomestic areas that can't be innately masculine.

Bane or Blessing?

During the seventies I have surveyed over 250 women who had never married and whose average age was in the early thirties. Generally their education extended beyond college and their vocations were semiprofessional or better. Among these women who had varied interests and environs, there was little difference in the proportion who thought being single carried more advantages than disadvantages and those who thought the reverse was true. Yet over 80 percent of them admitted that they felt that singles were stigmatized in our society. Before we judge them paranoid or hypersensitive, take note of the fact that several social analysts have been saying that our society does indeed make it difficult to be single. It even creates distressful situations which help promote the self-doubts and insecurities we will discuss in a later chapter.

Far from being distorted in their view of their social

situations or themselves, the never-married women I have talked with across many states have shown considerable insight into their frustrations and satisfactions alike. The "big three" problems for them appeared to be entertainment, sexual, and financial frustrations, in that order but differing very little in significance. You readers who are single will probably have to admit that even if going unescorted to public theaters or other places of entertainment and leisure does not make you uncomfortable or embarrassed, it is often impractical and even unsafe to do so. Very few of those with whom I have discussed the problems of recreation and excursions said they never felt like "fifth wheels" in social situations. Most of us find it easier to entertain even our couple friends in our apartments or homes rather than face the ordeal of a waiter who simply must give the bill to the man at the table, even when he is obviously not the host!

Since both married and single persons discuss sexual matters and problems more openly these days, it is not surprising that a majority of the unmarried women (69 percent) admitted that they experienced sexual frustration. However, only 8 percent felt great frustration and only about one third (35 percent) counted sex among their most pressing concerns. We might as well be candid about the fact that we live not only in a marrying society, but in a highly stimulating culture with respect to sex. Most products from lawnmowers to deodorants are advertised in sensuous contexts. Every contemporary novel, movie, or television program seems to be saturated with sexual episodes or stimulating references. We Americans have not seemed to take sex as a matter-of-fact, important but not idealized behavior. Some of my European friends have expressed amusement over our proneness to be exhibitionists or to give sex exaggerated significance in our lives. Consequently, the more mature single women I know are open about the fact that their celibacy has not erased their basic sexual drives or needs.

I am fully aware that many psychiatrists and medical doctors might recommend that a young woman who is not getting married would be better off to have a love affair or consider intermittent sexual encounters rather than fantasize or romanticize about sex. The subsequent hang-ups and guilt feelings, however, that might come to a girl of strong religious and moral convictions concerning premarital or casual sex would be disastrous if she followed such advice. In a recent conference with nearly 300 single women I heard them talking about the many subtle and forceful temptations to rationalize occasional sexual encounters, whether intentional or "accidental." While not a one was willing to state that nonmarital sex was the unpardonable or "original" sin, there was almost equal unanimity that neither should the church establish a double standard in its teaching about moral purity for the sake of singles. Besides that, the singles who have had affairs and those who have not seem to recognize that these involvements are often more frustrating and abusive than celibacy.

What then? A single woman represents a definite challenge to some single and married men alike. It is not necessary for you as a single woman to become wary and develop a set of obvious protective tactics to turn off improper advances or propositions. Learn to appreciate the difference between the genuine compliment of a male's attention or commendation and an invitation to an undesirable relationship. With good humor and tact, develop a firm but inoffensive manner of avoiding or "cooling off" a situation without making a scene. Look at your own actions and determine what you may be doing to precipitate unwelcome or unwise male attentions. Make sure you are not secretly enjoying any opportunity to prove that you are attractive and can say no at will!

A minority of women choose the alternative of unusually close relationships with other women and find that homosexuality is as unacceptable and unrewarding as heterosexual love trysts. Women who are not inclined to be lesbians may fall into homosexual relationships because they are not discovering better love outlets and are starved for close companionship. Take an honest look at yourself and see if you are investing your love in all of the available and acceptable manners. It was extremely interesting to me that almost 60 percent of the single women I talked to felt that being restricted sexually tended to make many singles more creative in other areas of their lives.

Least problematic among the top three areas of concern for these women was religion. Rather, they felt that being single afforded many opportunities for growth and greater varieties of professional and religious involvement. Practically none of them indicated that they missed the maternal role, but instead enjoyed the independence which permitted them to move vocationally and geographically. They placed special value on their friendships. If they were occasionally "moody," it was not due to their marital status or worry about whether they would someday marry. On the whole, they demonstrated keen insight into the strengths and the handicaps in their life-styles. Above all, they possessed strong self-concepts.

Perhaps the positive self-image of these nonmarrieds was related to an identification with the church. Almost three fourths of them felt that their churches did not discriminate against them. They did miss being included in the "family affairs" promoted by the church. Again, the taboos against premarital sex and casual bed-hopping were as valid to them as those against wife-swapping or married swinging. Over and over they, along with the bachelors, did verbalize their desire for unique programs for singles without the stigma of being "singled out" from all-church functions.

Contradictory myths have been abroad about marriage and singleness. "Marriage is the utopia of happiness and security" is as fallacious a statement as "singleness is free from responsibilities and problems." Each is a unique option of life with many varying life-styles, each having its own species of assets and liabilities. Some of the most content, loving, mature individuals are not married. The reverse is also true. Being an old maid is a state of mind as possible for the married as for the unmarried woman.

Some Helpful Readings About the Never-Marrieds

Adams, Margaret. "The Single Women in Today's Society," *The American Journal of Orthopsychiatry*, 1971, XLI, 776-86.

Andrews, Gini. *Your Half of the Apple*. Family Concern, Inc., Box 4249, Omaha, Nebraska; or Zondervan Press.

Bernard, Jessie. *The Future of the Family*. Bantam Books, 1973.

Glick, Paul C. "Bachelors and Spinsters," in Jeffrey Hadden & Marie Borgatta (eds.) *Marriage and the Family*, Peacock, 1969.

Greer, Rebecca. *Why Isn't a Nice Girl Like You Married?* Macmillan, 1969.

Jacoby, Susan. "49 Million Singles Can't Be All Right," *The New York Times Magazine*, February 17, 1974.

Jepson, Sarah. *For the Love of Singles*. Creation House, 1970.

Narramore, Clyde M. *The Unmarried Woman*. Zondervan, 1961.

Passin, Herbert. "The Single Past Imperfect," *Single* I, August, 1973.

Stein, Peter J. "Singlehood: An Alternative to Marriage," *The Family Coordinator* XXIV, October 1975, 489-503.

4
The Many Faces of the Nonmarried Ms: The Formerly Married

"Only the names were changed to protect" the once-married women whose real-life situations were among those described briefly at the beginning of the last chapter. How do you who are single *again* differ from those who are single *still*? Is there a common bond that binds together all of the formerly-married women with an inevitable gulf separating them from the nonexperienced? Not necessarily. There may be differences in typical age, life-style, and problems as we shall see in these three major groups of formerly married women.

Divorcee: Freedom from What?

In only one short generation the social situation for the divorcee has become much brighter and more accepting. Like death, divorce is not a respecter of sex nor does it generate too much public sympathy even today. But the divorced woman is not carrying the major protion of the burden and ensuing social problems as she once did. Presumably there is about equal feeling of disaster for husband and wife following a divorce now, spelled out in varying amounts of rejection, loneliness, guilt, and shame.

Women still initiate the divorce proceedings in the vast majority of cases, but usually after collusion or talking it over and agreeing on matters before the actual court hearing. Post-decree adjustment will not end as quickly or as often in remarriage for her as for her former spouse. If she does remarry, it will not be for almost five years while her ex-mate will do so within half that time. Part of this is due to the presence of children. The mother will generally get custody of them, and this fact may be a deterrent to remarriage.

Everyone these days seems to accept the situation in which the grounds for the divorce seldom coincide with the actual reason for the dissolution of the relationship. Actual reasons for divorce, however, are very much related to the subsequent adjustment and new life-style for the divorcee. If you are getting a divorce, the reasons are probably even more diverse and nebulous than the reasons a person remains single. This is largely due to the obvious fact that divorce involves couple situations as well as your individual traits and preferences.

No doubt one explanation for the brighter prospects for divorcees is their growing number. It may not be much comfort to know that there are more than three million other women sharing your marital failure and adjustment difficulties or that almost one million more will join your ranks this year. But it does have some effect on the reaction of society and even the church to your plight. A total of five million divorced persons constitutes a very visible group with rather predictable needs and tensions. The proportion of church-affiliates among them is no longer significantly different from the married population; certainly not whether they had a church wedding or not!

For several years now the number of persons whose marriages are terminated by divorce or annulment has been more than one third of the number getting married. The median duration of these marriages that are legally dissolved remains, however, about seven years. While many of these divorcees experience great relief from tense marital situations, it usually appears that they have "freedom from" without "freedom to." As one contemporary author of a best-seller on the problems of divorce has said, divorce may be "an exchange of chains." In a sense, it is a defeat that cannot be turned into a victory, although one may learn to cope with the pain and feelings of "oddness."

Being divorced can mean being fettered to economic, sexual, and religious problems that erupt from the interrupted regimen of marriage, even an unhappy one. There is sometimes an accompanying feeling of hypocrisy because the grounds used were the best legal possibility, though hardly the actual ones. Guilt is also to be reckoned with when one can't offer a concrete major factor for the split-up—such as brutality, lack of support, or drunkenness—because the intolerable situation was an accumulation of "minor" greivances or alienation. Perhaps divorce occurs because the two people married to each other changed and grew, no longer the two individuals who made their vows and no longer compatible. Frankly, much morbidity and self-pity on the part of a divorcee may be because her closest associates regard the action as reprehensible and irresponsible.

One psychiatrist has negated the need to dwell on the painful "why?" of divorce. Once the individual moves on to a more positive "why not?"—particularly under the circumstances—she may then start rebuilding her life. This same therapist has seriously questioned the possibility of the friendly divorce. One may agree that divorce should end all the hostility and unresolved differences, but it is common knowledge that it seldom does. The notion that one can, simply by decree, slip overnight from bitterness and sparring into a benevolent, accepting friendliness with a former spouse puts a strain on credibility. Either the marriage was all along a shallow, peripheral relationship or a woman must admit that she is adept at self-deception and sham. Particularly if you have strong religious convictions, as a divorcee you may feel guilty that you cannot feel forgiving and wipe the slate clean in order to start a new life. You may need professional help to see your own mistakes in the relationship and to begin the healing process.

Adjustment to a nonmarried relationship with a former mate is often necessary when both continue to live in the same community or children are involved. It may be made easier when remarriage occurs for both partners and there are no children, but this does not involve an overwhelming number of divorced couples. Remarriage itself becomes a serious moral and religious dilemma for those who considered the divorce as the very last resort in a bad marriage. The problems faced by the mother without a partner will be dealt with in a later chapter, with particular attention directed toward "unmanned" children and Saturday fathers.

More crucial than wounded pride for the divorcee is the feeling of economic inexperience, especially if she has not been a working wife. Moving out into the business and professional world where other women of the same age and education may already have experienced achievement and prestige can be a humbling experience. The beginning salary may not support the standard of living to which a wife has been accustomed. Balancing the new single homelife with adjustments on a new job may be overwhelming. Divorce may cause a real financial crisis, eating up a large portion of individual or couple savings depending on who files for the divorce. Recent estimates indicate the minumum fee may be $350 when a lawyer represents both husband and wife, but it can reach as much as $1,000 each in an uncontested case or up to $5,000 each in a contested divorce. Since the average working wife earns an income which is only 60 percent of her husband's income, assuming a part or all of the legal costs may be worse than an unexpected hospitalization expense would be. The equitable distribution of the furniture and mementos of several years in shared living can be as much of an emotional drain as a financial crisis.

As I have reviewed almost 150 cases of divorcees in my files, I found that financial frustrations were only the number two problem. Probably because they were about ten years older than singles I had interviewed, even with slightly less education, they were faring considerably better in salaries. Indeed, they were approaching the median income for the entire population. If they had custody of any children, they would still not enjoy that much more buying power.

Reflecting the lingering scars attached to divorce and the presence of children, the number one frustration for my sample of divorcees was entertainment. Finding acceptable social outlets was twice as great a problem as sexual or children problems. Unlike singles, they felt their current life-styles had greater disadvantages than assets and 97 percent of them felt "somewhat" to "greatly" stigmatized. The majority admitted that they experienced some sexual frustrations. Also about half indicated that being divorced produced some work liabilities. One of the supportive aspects of their lives appeared to be their perception of their church or religion as being tolerant and accepting of the divorced person. Less than one third felt that they had been treated differently, as if they were an abnormal church member. The redemptive mission of the church appeared to have been working for most of these formerly marrieds.

Separation: Women in Limbo

Women who are separated form a precarious marital group, difficult to enumerate accurately and more difficult to characterize. If you are separated from your mate, your sisters number around 2.5 million, but this is at best a "guesstimate," since the number of separated men does not agree with the figures for separated women! A difference of several hundred thousand women over men indicates faulty perception, among even those involved, concerning the definition of separation. Exclusive of those couples who are living apart due to military service, hospitalization, or similar causes, this marital category embraces women whose husbands have deserted them (and may periodically return), as well as the legal and interim (trial) separations. However one labels the separated woman, she lives in a state of limbo—psychologically, physically, and legally. She is not living in a marital relationship yet there is no legal decree terminating the marriage.

A woman whose husband has deserted her is often in a situation akin to the wife of a gambler or alcoholic. Her problem is a chronic one since deserters are frequently repeaters. The emotional and financial drain of living in such a yo-yo relationship is hard to exaggerate. As chairman of our Church Ministries Committee in my local church, I recall vividly the ministry of our church people to two women with eight and nine children, living borderline existences while the fathers-husbands came and went at will. Outside concern can only provide Band-Aid assistance until such a woman realizes that therapy will help her understand why she tolerates, by choice or need, such a life-style. The saying "I can cope with anything but uncertainty" has special meaning for this woman. If she has a neurotic need to experience this pattern of spasmodic marriage, she must be helped to examine her priorities when the needs of any children are involved.

A large number of divorces are preceded by one or more periods of separation. These are mostly "bed and board" separation and some have little aura of finality about them. Occasionally reconciliation occurs—more often divorce is the end result. Studies have indicated that one out of every three couples have considered separation in the early tentative and vulnerable years of their marriage. A pastor of a medium-sized church recently confided that his counseling contacts alone made him aware of at least six under thirty-five married couples (with children) who had been "off-again, on-again" more than three times during the past two years of his ministry. There is reason to believe that this is true of most congregations where couples are pressured to try again and again before making it legal and final.

Legal separation involves a mutual agreement on domiciles, support, and property settlements, as well as child custody. It may put the woman in a relatively fixed marital limbo, because the couple wishes to avoid divorce on religious, professional, or other personal grounds. It is often referred to as a partial divorce and obviously the woman (or man) is not free to remarry.

All types of separation can lead a woman to be uncertain and insecure. It may have all of the problems of divorce with few of the assets. Community agencies that serve the family will find the counseling of the separated an integral and supportive part of this program. As in the case of the therapy of alcoholics, nothing may be more supportive to the separated than one who "has been there." It is significant that in the survey of unmarried women a greater proportion of separted women felt ignored by the church, but less by society in general, than did the singles or divorced.

The Universal Uncoupler

As sober as it may sound, to go on being married (happily or so-so) is to eventually have your marriage interrupted by death. The grim reaper is no respecter of persons, though it seems to reap more heavily in the older, more durable marriages. There is an increasing number of young widows, though, who have lost their husbands through death. For every separated woman there are approximately five widows and for every divorcee there are at least three widows, so death is statistically and emotionally probably the single most disruptive factor in American marriage.

Unlike many less "civilized" societies, however, our society affords no sure guidelines for handling grief and loss. Our culture seems to think death will go away, or at least its sting will, if you ignore it or fail to treat it realistically. This has encouraged a host of disguise phrases about the reality of death: She has passed away; Papa is asleep for a long nap; Brother has gone away to be with God. Even the religious employ such verbal devices to avert the finality and universality of death.

The widow is showered with attention and support during the first few weeks following the death of her spouse, but her numbness at this stage renders her only semiconscious of others' concern and the decisions yet to be made. By the time every nerve has awakened to the pain of bereavement, not only is the funeral director gone, but also the minister, relatives, and friends who had to get back to their normal routine. Neither the saccharine funeral home booklets nor the memories of spoken bromides seem to relieve the paranoid panic that sets in. Alone. Not loved well enough. Guilty memories about the dead. Anger at God. Self-pity. Negative emotions run a vicious circle as they have to be directed outward—toward children who seem to recover too quickly, toward friends who seem heartless in their frequent unavailability, toward the deceased for not taking preventative steps, toward God for letting it all happen. The harshness of being called a "widow," such a hollow, something's-missing sound. But the "widow" isn't dead, she's painfully alive.

The bereaved need a counselor, lawyer, economist, crying-shoulder, and friends as the six-weeks to six-months of panic merges into restorative adjustment. The church may be a major agent as the healing process takes place. Over twenty years ago, a study of mine concerned various types of "church families" and revealed that widows, even then a growing segment of most congregations, were a forgotten minority. There were few, if any, continuing or long-term programs for the bereaved. One of the most successful programs in recent years is the widow-to-widow ministry, in which a woman who has worked through grief to acceptance and new areas of fulfillment provides support to a new widow. Grief is a necessary healing process, but counsel is needed in all of the decisions to be made for a new life-style.

Self-concept is a crucial aspect of survival in widowhood. Some women equate "widow" with growing old, being dependent, and having life pass them by. Being with men, family, or friends is an important aspect of accommodating to bereavement but it must not make one develop an enduring and premature dependence on such a helpful male. Taking stock of one's talents and interests is the preliminary step to getting involved in meaningful hobbies, organizations, and even work. No better therapy can be found than good reading, stimulating educational programs, or helping someone or some group in straitened circumstances.

The average widow can expect about a decade of widowhood, or five years plus the difference in ages of the married couple. Poor investments, rushing to join various superficial social organizations, and other decisions made in haste can have many tragic repercussions for months and years to come. Waiting as much as one can on important business matters until the accommodation period is reached is wise counsel. Death and funeral expenses can easily average $5,000 and careful managing is necessary for a widow to make insurance and widow's benefits from Social Security suffice until she can become more self-supporting.

If you are recently widowed, be assured that these observations concerning the widow are intended to be realistic, but not pessimistic. Indeed, you may find that the adjustment process is easier for the bereaved than for the divorced in that society is much more sympathetic and tolerant toward the widowed. There is usually less aura of defeat, failure, and shame for you. The divorcee has less certainty in her social roles. There is comfort in the knowledge that women in general adjust more completely and healthily than do men, even though they have less chance for remarriage.

In a recent conference for nonmarried women, it was significant that only a little over 17 percent of almost 500 women who attended were widows. A partial explanation for their proportionately smaller group in comparison to the divorcees might be their age bracket. Their average age was about fifty-two, whereas the average divorcee was forty-one years of age. Those who did attend reflected better adjustment to their status than did the divorced. Although the widows felt more at odds in a married society, they felt considerably less maligned than the divorcees. They were realistic about their mood changes being related to their bereavement, but they felt that their future happiness was not dependent on remarriage. The vast majority felt that their marital status did not work against them on the job or in the church. However, it is significant that even one third of them felt that they were treated differently as church members.

And So . . .

While the single, divorced, and widowed may share aloneness, they are unique in their social and spiritual needs. A desire for a wider social life is a common denominator for all of them, but the kind of entertainment and circle of friends desired by the fifty-year-old widow is quite different from the social life that would appeal to a twenty-four-year-old single girl or the thirty-three-year-old divorcee. Regardless of their age or status, they will usually outnumber the unmarried men, so leisure activities must offer companionship without providing romance in every instance.

Some Books for the Formerly Married

Separated

Baguedor, Eve. *Separation Journal of a Man*. New York: Simon & Schuster, 1972.

Widowed

Bolgum, David. *Alone, Alone, All All Alone*. Family Concern, Inc., Box 4249, Omaha, Nebraska.

Caine, Lynn. *Widow*. William Morrow & Company, Inc., 1974.

Silverman, Phyllis Rolfe. "The Widow to Widow Program," *Mental Hygiene* LIII (July 69) 333-37.

Start, Clarissa. *On Becoming a Widow*. New York Family Library Pyramid Publications, 1973.

Switzer, David. *The Dynamics of Grief*. Nashville: Abingdon Press, 1970.

Divorced

Abraxas Corp. *Marriage & Divorce*. Los Angeles, 1974 (journal).

Block, Jean Libman. *Back in Circulation*. New York: Macmillan, 1969.

Bohanan, Paul ed. *Divorce and After*. New York: Doubleday, 1970.

Galloway, Dale E. *Dream a New Dream*. Family Concern, Inc., Box 4249, Omaha, Nebraska.

Hirsch, Barbara. *Divorce for Women*. Chicago: Henry Regnery, 1973.

Hudson, Luther R. *'Til Divorce Do Us Part*. Nashville: Thomas Nelson, 1973.

Krantzler, Mel. *Creative Divorce*. New York: M. Evans Co., 1973.

Sherwin, Robert V. *Compatible Divorce*. Crown Publishers New York, 1969.

Stewart, Suzanne. *Divorced! "I Wouldn't Have Given a Nickel for Your Chances."* Zondervan, 1974.

General

Athearn, Louise M. *What Every Formerly Married Woman Should Know*. McKay, 1973.

Donelson, Kenneth and Irene. *Married Today, Single Tomorrow*. New

York: Doubleday & Co., Inc., 1969.
Hunt, Morton M. *The World of the Formerly Married*. McGraw-Hill, 1966.
Lyman, Howard B. *Single Again*. David McKay Co., 1971.

5
Mother Without Father

The solo parent, whether mother or father, usually feels there are unique adjustments to be made to living without a partner. Not only must the search for personal identity and satisfying life-style be under way, but all present and future plans carry the additional responsibility of insuring that one's offspring mature as normally as possible without the other adult model. Certainly all two-parent families don't provide the best possible models and growing environment for children; but a parent alone feels especially self-conscious about the sobering challenge of providing all of the trappings of a happy childhood.

In only five years' time during the early 1970's the number of households headed by mothers has increased from one out of ten to one out of eight. To put it more strongly, during the last decade, homes with solo mothers grew ten times faster than husband-wife families. Almost 15 percent of America's children under eighteen (about 9 million) are going to be growing up with primarily a female parent-image. There are many varied reasons for an absent father—death, divorce, desertion, marital/occupational/institutional separation, unwed pregnancy, or adoption by a single woman. Nothing is universally true about these mothers.

There is no single prototype in family adjustments that

we can propose even within a particular category of solo mothers. A recent widow with college offspring faces quite different adjustment problems than the thirty-year-old war widow with two children under school age. If you are a divorcee with a six-year-old son, you can anticipate different problems to solve than the woman with a sixteen-year-old daughter or one with four teenage boys and girls. Certain general observations can be made about mothers without fathers, however. They are much more numerous than solo fathers and most of them will have to work outside the home because child-support is minimal or nonexistent. Such work will usually earn subaverage income; therefore, the budget may be tight and the living arrangements crowded and insecure. A disproportionate number of single mothers come from minority groups, but the number of white, middle-class, church-affiliated, and well-educated solo mothers has been growing.

In the Beginning . . .

Whatever has disrupted the family with children, most women will experience some self-negating feelings during the first few months of living alone with the children. It is not a time when logical reasoning comes easily. Coping with these negative emotions can be an isolating, embittering period or it can be a growth interval as one assesses how much there is to live for and how many depend on your positive adjustment.

Grief.—Bereavement can be present as much in divorce, separation, and desertion as it is in the death of a spouse. There is small comfort in knowing that probably one third of the adult women in America have experienced a similar grief experience. Grief is a unique, highly intimate, and walled-in feeling. It can be bottled-up or released in tears and hostility. It can even be nursed along with self-pity and withdrawal.

Most grief passes through stages—numbness, confused panic, and the final search for a well-adjusted life-style. A divorced or deserted mother often will not experience the comforting, protective support of the widowed mother during the numb phase. With or without kindly concern, this is not a good time for making decisions of long-range significance. It is also very easy to shut out one's children and forget that grief is not an exclusive, adult experience. The shared sense of loss among the remaining family members can aid the healing process and bind them together in a new kind of closeness.

The state of confused panic follows, and it produces different anxieties in different women. A sympathetic public has gone its way, back to daily routine matters while there are all sorts of loose ends to gather up and reweave into a meaningful family life. One mother may discover how woefully uninformed she is about the financial state of affairs; another wakes up to the fact that she has virtually no activities or interests outside the home that were not shared with her husband. Some may need to brush up on rusty work skills and get emotionally "psyched-up" for moving out into the labor force from which they have been detached for years. Holding the reins on self-debasing tendencies while one assesses the situation is a must. The natural anxiety of "can I go it alone?" should gradually grow into the kind of confidence that asserts, "I am of value; I do have some innate abilities; I can achieve mastery of this situation for myself and my children."

Denial and repression.—Frequently even when a woman admits openly that a marriage is over, terminated by death or desire, there still may be a reluctance to confront the reality of the absence of the partner and the adjustments to be made. This is what our younger generation would rather brutally call a cop-out reaction. It certainly has the effect of postponing necessary decisions and of delaying the formation of some new routine of living. But I have seen countless simple decisions and transactions become complicated while the female head of the family refused to admit that she now must take charge.

Clark Hensley in his *Help for Single Parents* has wisely observed that two of our most important and blessed faculties are memory and imagination. But these can work for or against adjustment in the postmarital period. It is good to recall the wonderful shared experiences of the deceased husband and to idealize the good moments before a marriage went bad. It can be a serious stumbling block to allow such memories to deter you from new and satisfying relationships with the children or new friends. To fantasize that a divorced spouse will "come to his senses" and return to his family may keep the remaining family in a destructive limbo that holds out false hope for the child.

Bewilderment.—Following the loss of any close associate and particularly a spouse, questions are raised which the heart believes the head can not really answer. "How could *our* marriage have failed?" "How could God take my husband when we seemed to be on the highest plateau of occupational and marital success?" "How do I sort out all the snarls and tangles this loss creates for me and my children?" "Why couldn't this have happened *after* we had reared the children?" "Could I honestly have handled it any better then?"

One must be careful that one's philosophy and theology of life do not suddenly warp at this crisis. It becomes very easy to attribute human frailities to God's whimsical control of human events or to explain a decade or more of accumulating factors of marital discord with one oversimplified "cause" of the divorce or separation. Verbalizing or even acting as if God or the spouse had no right to do these things to you can make a lasting and detrimental impression on youthful minds. Bewilderment can be a contagious environment for children, as can these other early reactions to loss.

Blame-guilt-defeat.—These are interlocking emotional reactions for the mother alone. They also operate in a vicious circle that is debilitating to a good adjustment and a new life-style with the children. Whether a widow blames herself that she did not protect her husband's health or she blames the deceased for ignoring her pleas that he slow down and spend more time on himself and the family, the subsequent guilt is equally demoralizing. Whether a woman feels that she forced her husband to stray away or blames him because he was irresponsible and walked away from a family he had pledged to care for and protect for the rest of his life, blame and guilt use up energy the widow needs for reconstructing her life.

Soul-searching for one's own limitations can be a first step to building a new identity and relationship with the children. Dwelling too long on "Where did I make a mistake?" "What's wrong with me that things don't go right?" breeds defeatism. And children can be very sensitive to a mother's implied belief that "nothing is going to go right for us again." Soul-searching about another's faults and hurtful behaviors should be dealth with quickly, if at all, and dismissed as nonproductive as one faces the future.

Shame.—Mothers and children alike experience embarrassment and shame following divorce, desertion, and illegitimacy. It matters little that society appears to be placing less stigma on the divorcee or unwed mother. What is important is what one feels in response to the situation. Sometimes the mothers who appear almost to flaunt their divorced or unwed status in the face of society and the church may be feeling the most acute anguish and humiliation.

A young single woman whom I had for years in Sunday School and had known in the community and college went off alone and unwed to have her baby. She chose to return with her son to her hometown, to her old job, and to college. There were mixed reactions from those who knew her—dismay, surprise, admiration, cynicism. She admitted to mixed emotions also—dogged determination, shame, protective love, ambition, and hope. Two years later the positive vibrations outweigh the negative ones, but she knows there are still hurdles to confront at every stage down the road. The church, family, and friends have been supportive, but it is still a lonely road at times . . . although the prognosis looks good.

Aching loneliness.—Single mothers do not have a monopoly on loneliness. But children can be a constant reminder of shared experiences in a marriage. This kind of painful vacuum can cause a woman to turn to numerous undesirable behaviors to try to fill up particularly the lonely hours of evening and nights when the children are with their own friends or in bed. A mother could come to rely too closely on the companionship of children and deny herself the company of her peers, as well as cut off the children from normal youth activities. There can be the temptation to become overly dependent on parents and relatives, who may be all too willing to help alleviate the loneliness and may be unaware of the dangers of "reattached umbilical cords."

One widower in my hometown a few years ago remarked with alarm and distaste about the number of widows and divorcees who began calling him almost immediately after his wife's death with invitations for a wide assortment of activities from coffee to suppers to weekend plans. Searching for any available male to fill the social void left by a husband not only may not solve the loneliness problem, it could well open a Pandora's box of new ones! Would four or five haphazardly chosen acquaintances really compensate for a lost and cherished companion?

There are many ways to turn loneliness into creative aloneness and some of these will be dealt with in another chapter. Certainly frenzied joining of organizations, creating meaningless "busy" work, or living vicariously through the children do not make for a satisfying life. One friend who has such a comfortable living afforded by her late husband that she makes several cross-nation and overseas trips each year admits that she still has not solved the basic problem of what to do with herself those few awful nights when she does come home to roost. Admitting all of this, what is one to do?

Taking Inventory Alone

Of yourself.—When the numbness and the bewildering stages begin to pass, the time comes for grasping what one knows of objectivity and for backing off to evaluate the assets and liabilities of the situation you now have and must live with. There's no place to begin but with yourself. Trite as it sounds, you are the only you. You, formerly one of a pair of parents, are now on your own. As mothers generally go, you probably always were responsible for a large part of the child-rearing, running the household, and possibly earning the living. So now it's all yours. But you have already proved that you are a *person* and one that has workable capacities.

Take as much time as you dare and read what other women have done in similar plights. The very fact some of you are reading this book is indication that you are on the right track for finding your unique solution to a problem many women have faced before you. Piece together your own patchwork quilt of advice and caution so that you can avoid the pitfalls in child-rearing, finances, work situations, running the house, or leisure activities that others have discovered.

Time is at best your servant; so rank order your time

priorities, lest it become your Minotaur. That marvelous and horrible monster of Greek mythology, pinioned in the canyons of the isle of Crete, was docile, only if it was fed prime subjects. Some decisions that involve housing, a job, or debts will have to be dealt with immediately. There is relatively more time for you to decide about long-range plans for the children such as college, part-time jobs, or summer camp. Many months and years may have to pass before wounds heal and you work out interrupted sexual and companionship regimens. In the meantime, doggedly tending to the immediate decisions and endeavoring to alleviate the pain in your child's life will assuage some of your emptiness and bring you surrogate pleasure.

Your child.—Children are not as fragile as adults often suppose. Most of them are amazingly resilient and can bounce back from physical disease or emotional trauma with almost as much speed as they fall prey to them. Approximately 90 percent of children of divorce are awarded to their mothers although there is no hard evidence to support the thesis that in today's society the mother is infinitely better equipped than the father to aid the restorative process for the child. The age, sex, personality, and prior parental relationships of each child would best determine the parent who should rear the child after divorce. Nevertheless, this is the general judicial perspective—mother knows best. In widowhood, there is no judge.

There is need to look at children thrust overnight into the one-parent situation with a fresh perspective. No two in the same family will react the same way to the absence of a father. While love and physical security must be supplied impartially, different coping tactics will have to be worked out as Mother supervises before and after school schedules, arranges visiting times with the father, and meets the emotional needs peculiar to each child. Generally, a child is buffered by the presence of several siblings. An only child will have, after all, lost one half his/her interpersonal potential in the family arena and may feel greater personal loss accordingly.

Remember the child did not divorce his father or wish him dead. Nevertheless, the animal desire to survive in a new situation (physical or emotional) will prompt most children to attempt to manipulate affairs to what they consider their best advantage. To allow the new family system to be restructured primarily or exclusively to children's wants or needs is unrealistic training for later years. Adjustment must be family-centered and not according to any individual's selfish demands—mother or child.

Your relationship to the father.—The "father" is still a person to be reckoned with even when he is no longer the husband-in-residence. His image to the divorcee or the widow may be tinged, even coated, with bitterness, anger, dislike, or repugnance. Whatever the justifications for these valid or contrived feelings toward the late spouse, it is important to see how damaging they are to one's well-being and efficiency. Considering what the mother faces, there is no time or place for this kind of ball and chain as one presses forward to wholesome family experience.

Keep a positive profile of the father before the children. Avoid placing blame on the divorced or dead spouse. Both idealization and denigration are dishonest. The young children will be bewildered and upset by either attitude; the older children will realize both shortcomings and virtues as they sort out the memories and current contacts with their father. Nothing will test your maturity more than this exercise in Christian charity.

Except in rare cases, father doesn't get equal exposure. As you work out divorce settlements, visitation rights are a number-one priority. Be open and equitable. Assuming the father is alive and really cares about his children, how would you feel if the roles were reversed? Insofar as is humanly possible, rise above pettiness and give him the benefit of the doubt—unless it becomes damaging to the child. Very early provide for a wide variety of associations with the living father. Being only with a Saturday Father can quickly become a stereotyped, unimaginative and parenthesis experience for everyone involved. Assure the child some holidays, birthdays, summer vacations, and weekends with their daddy whenever possible. It is important that parents agree that gifts and trips will be discussed and determined with consideration for what is best for the child's welfare and not either parent's ego.

If the father is deceased, talk about pleasant shared experiences and memories easily and frequently. Encourage others who knew him well to talk about his life and happenings in the presence of the children. Keep family pictures which include him around the home. Point out positive physical and personality traits in the children which are similar to those in their father. This can be as supportive to the mother as to the children.

Your financial picture.—When death or divorce comes, a working mother shifts quickly from "contribution" to the financial status of the family to "economic head" of the household. Almost inevitably becoming a solo mother means serious setbacks in the financial picture of the family. Over one half of the women who head households will get no child support following divorce and many will have inadequate insurance after the death of the spouse. About one fourth of the fatherless families fall below poverty level.

Although a large number of women pay the family bills and do the routine shopping for clothing, groceries, and notions, you as a mother alone may discover that you are uninformed on buying and maintaining a house or car, carrying adequate life and health insurance, or investing wisely. Indeed, many women will work in positions that do not carry the same pension, hospitalization, and fringe benefit plans that men's jobs would have. Sex discrimination in the work world is still to be reckoned with in both salary and fringe benefits.

One of the earliest changes may have to come in the size and location of the family home. In order to economize, you may want a smaller home closer to work or the children's school. A suburban home may not seem so advantageous when one needs to save travel time, gas money, and cut out one family car. If there is need to retrain or update work skills, some of the husband's insurance may have to be invested in college or trade school programs as well as carrying the family through this interim period before mother brings in an income.

The big four budget items will probably not change with the loss of the father—food, shelter, clothing, and transportation. The more a working mother has to pay others to make or service her family's goods, the tighter the budget will be. Ready-prepared food, clothes off the rack, and child care cost considerably more than when these needs are supplied at home. If there are preschool children, good but reasonably priced day care is difficult to find. There must be a careful weighing of more literate teachers in a group care center against less trained and less expensive sitters who give individual care in the home. Not only must a mother pay for things she once provided her family, but she may now have to pay for yard care, cleaning house gutters, and even minor repairs that the husband had cared for.

Your relatives.—Maintaining your equilibrium with kin after you lose a spouse can be a challenge. Even though relatives tend to be a scattered species in this generation, rapid transportation and the phone can make you walk precariously between their loving, inquisitive intrusion and your temptation to rely heavily on their advice and generosity. Of course, sometimes they can be brutally critical of how you manage alone. It is also possible that you may impose on nearby grandparents for baby-sitting or male help in repairs around the house.

Keeping a close relationship between your children and their paternal relatives is not always possible, but the positive image you want them to have of their father is linked with his family. In-laws do not usually deserve the reputation they are given, but sometimes they can bear ill-will toward the daughter-in-law about the death of their son or place blame for the wrecked marriage on her. Attempts at compromise and tolerance are worthy, however, when the alternative is alienation. Firm but kind stands on the discipline and gifts given the children by grandparents and other relatives should be taken at the outset—it prevents hard feelings and strained relationships later. There are no carbon copies in three-generational family patterns—find the one that produces harmony and utility for your particular situation.

Your extra-familial life.—One of the most difficult areas of adjustment for the solo mother is finding time for and comfort in the social groups once shared with her husband. Even sitting in church alone when the youngsters are scattered across the sanctuary with their friends can be an excruciating experience. The "fifth-wheel" syndrome can be present even when it comes to visiting in the homes of couple friends or attending organizational meetings. There is a temptation to become a social drop-out or to become preoccupied with chauffering children to their activities and supervising teenage ventures. When the empty nest stage comes then, mother is bereft beyond measure.

The other extreme is to join all manner of clubs and groups promiscuously—anything to keep busy and not be home alone. For this person, there may be a dozen well-meaning acquaintances who are eager to matchmake. Rushing headlong into a hodgepodge of activities is an exercise in futility and may seriously shortchange the quality time you have with the children. Try to budget your time among the children's needs, time with close friends, some select interest or hobby involvements, church and service projects. Giving all of your time to any one, no matter how demanding or interesting, may limit your growth in this adjustment period. Move carefully; it is more difficult to get uninvolved than to begin an activity or join a group!

A great many communities offer a unique opportunity for the single mother or father to have association with other solo parents through the organization Parents Without Partners. There are over 800 chapters scattered throughout all of the states, so that there would probably be one in a nearby metropolitan community if there is none in yours. These groups provide a nonsectarian, educational setting for sharing strengths and problem areas in the one-parent household. A wide variety of programs and services are available through its volunteer, nonprofit activities. There are also social activities that are both adult and family oriented. Its magazine, *The Single Parent*, touches on every conceivable interest and need of the parent who is committed to providing a normal and happy environment not only for her fatherless children, but for herself as well.

Readings for Mother Without Father

Bernstein, Rose. *Helping Unmarried Mothers*. Association Press, 1970.

Despert, J. Louise. *Children of Divorce*. Doubleday and Co., 1962.

Douglas, William. *The One-Parent Family*. Nashville: Graded Press, 1971 (Methlodist Publishing House).

Grollman, Earl A., ed. *Explaining Death to Children*. Boston: Beacon Press, 1967.

Hallett, Kathryn J. *ATA Primer for the Single Parent*. St. Louis, Mo: Transactional Analyst, 1973.

Hallett, Kathryn. *A Guide for Single Parents: People in Crisis*. Celestial Arts, 1974.

Hensley, J. Clark. *Help for Single Parents*. Christian Action Com., M. B. C., Jackson, Miss., 1973.

Jackson, Edgar N. *Telling a Child About Death*. Hawthorn Books, 1965.

Klein, Carole. *The Single Parent Experience*. Walker & Co., 1973.

LeMasters, E. E. *Parents in Modern America*. Dorsey Press, 1970, Chapter 9.

Mindey, Carol. *The Divorced Mother*. New York: McGraw-Hill, 1970.

Parents Without Partners. *The Best from the Single Parent*. Washington, D. C., 1973.

Pierce, Ruth I. *Single and Pregnant*. Beacon Press, 1971.

Ross, Heather L. & Isabel V. Sawhill. *Time of Transition—The Growth of Families Headed by Women*. Washington, D. C.: The Urban Institute, 1976.

The Single Parent, The Journal of Parents Without Partners, Inc., 7910 Nordment Ave., Washington, D. C.

Schlesinger, Benjamin. *The One-Parent Family*. University of Toronto, 1975.

Steinzor, Bernard. *When Parents Divorce*. Panthean Books, 1969.

Switzer, David K. *The Dynamics of Grief*. Abingdon Press, 1976.

Taves, Isabella. *Women Alone*. New York: Funk & Wagnalls, 1969.

Vayhinger, John M. *The Single Parent Family*. Nashville: Board of Education, Methodist Church., 1972.

Wolf, Anna W. M. & Stein, Lucille. *The One-Parent Family*. Public Affairs Pamphlet #287, 1975.

6
Ten Commandments for a Solo Mother

No one would dare presume to draw a blueprint for being an effective parent without a partner because no two households will have the same characteristics and needs. Nevertheless there are some obvious desirable parenting commonalities to be hoped for and worked at. Consider at least the following ten "musts" in your mother-child relationships:

1. *Protect the child from undue negative emotional "fallout" following the loss of the father.* The child should never get the feeling that he/she is to some extent responsible for the death or the divorce. To adult reasoning this may seem an absurd likelihood, but in a young child's fantasies and feelings it can sometimes happen and bring about unnecessary guilt.

There will be differences in a youngster's sense of emptiness and loss, of course, depending on whether it follows death or divorce. Even though young children may have encountered dying and grief via television, nursery stories, family pets, or the loss of a grandparent, losing a dad is a very special bereavement that must express itself emotionally more than rationally. Dealing calmly with a child's acting out in anger, fear, or possessiveness may strain a mother's own emotional discipline to the ultimate, but it is important to provide a secure comfort from the one remaining parent. Forcing a child to go to the funeral to "see daddy for the last time" may be an unrealistic and traumatic demand. Speak of the death in honest, matter-of-fact terms and answer the child's questions without confusing or complicated theological and biological explanations. There is a special bond of intimacy that can come to a mother and child when they have shared such a sadness, and memories of a mother who had courage in the face of deep personal loss will carry over into adulthood.

When divorce removes the constant association with a father, there may be need for assurance that the child's own mischief or misbehavior did not cause the father to leave or the marriage to suffer. Insofar as possible a child needs to understand that both parents may sincerely wish that it need not be so for the child's sake. But stress that parental love does not have to be "in residence" and that the father will continue to be concerned for his children. It will be helpful if both parents have talked with the child before the father leaves and if there is complete freedom for him to talk with the child by phone between visits.

2. *Don't assume and behave as if a one-parent household has to shortchange your child's growth and development.* Nor is it predestined to provide only a negative model for later courtship and marriage experiences. Family and child development specialists have been saying for several decades now that a happy, fulfilled solo parent provides a much better growing environment than a mediocre, strained, or hostile two-parent household. A single parent can meet the needs of a child if they can meet their own. A very important "if" is the mother's own sense of fulfillment and adjustment to aloneness.

It is ridiculous to expect to be both a mother and a father to your children. Of course, there will be new tasks to perform that once the male adult took care of but there is no need to so tightly define parent roles in terms of "mothering" and "fathering." Assuming these extra family functions will take additional time slots in your schedule so there is more pressure for quality time when the relationship is uniquely mother-child. Just as you can not expect to be "father" to your children, it is no more realistic to expect television, toys, extra clubs, or special lessons to become substitute fathers. A child can accommodate to a missing relationship better than he can accept the fact that a remaining relationship is not all that it should or can be. Children are amazingly adept at working to make the one-to-one relationship they have left happy and satisfying if they know the mother is. The important thing to remember is there is a happy median ground for both mother and child between smothering and benign neglect.

3. *Show your respect for your children as persons by including them in the plans for your collective future.* Even when you reserve the last word by virtue of more maturity and experience, acknowledge their investment in your new family life-style as you work out plans such as where to live, whether you will work, changes in schools, adjustments in finances. You can share what must be decided without burdening them beyond their age and abilities. Be cautious about calling the oldest son the "head of the household" or the oldest daughter the "housekeeper" or "second mother" to the younger children even though you will be encouraging all to be a part of the working team to make successful adjustments in the new situation.

As you share the financial situation of the family without painting a hopeless or bleak picture, there will be very good learning situations for the children with respect to the wise use of money. Perhaps there is truth in Somerset Maugham's observation in *Of Human Bondage*, "There is nothing so degrading as the constant anxiety about one's means of livelihood . . . Money is like a sixth sense without which you cannot make complete use of the other five."

If the children have not been on an allowance plan, begin now to teach them how to make decisions and manage their own money. As they grow older gradually include things other than school supplies, lunch money, and recreation in their money management. Let them assume more and more responsibility for spending their own clothing and activities funds. Consider the possibility of earning roles outside the home on a part-time basis. Be careful that you do not "pay" for tasks which they should view as their natural responsibilities in the keeping of the family household—"doing" dishes, keeping their rooms and clothes, nonspecialized maintenance of things around the house and yard, running errands, helping each other. Even when the incomplete family is still relatively affluent, children should not grow up with the expectation that everything is being provided or done for them.

4. *Provide the security of firm, consistent, and appropriate discipline.* There is no reason to expect the same disciplinary approaches that work in a two-parent family not to be workable for a mother alone. Reasonable, certain rewards and punishment are the right of every child; they are the greatest assurance of love and concern. It is disastrous to all relationships if mother and father do not agree on and practice the same discipline when the child is with either of them. Being unusually permissive in order to gain the favor of the child is doing the child no favor in future growth and development. It does not even work toward long-range respect for that parent.

You are the child's greatest model for equity and justice. Base the meeting of punishment and the withdrawal of privileges on clear understanding of the cause and effect patterns in his future behavior. Make children aware that they are loved even when they do mischievous and unacceptable things, that you care too much about them to let harmful behaviors go unnoticed and unrebuked. Help them to internalize standards of right and wrong so that they do not have to depend on mother's conscience and presence in order to act appropriately. I remember when my godson reached the point when he literally was miserable until he reported some unknown misbehavior, not because he had an overactive superego or a compulsion to be punished but because he needed the confession and catharsis of telling someone who cared before he could carry through on "being sorry" and changing the situation!

5. *Encourage peer group participation both in and outside the home.* It is no more healthy for your child to spend most of his/her nonschool time with you and other adults than it is for you to have only the company of your children. There should be adequate involvement in both organized and informal age-group activities. You do not have to turn your household into Grand Central Station for Little People in order to provide the warmth and welcome for the friends of your children to gather often in the privacy of their own rooms or with the entire family. Learning to accept responsibilities as members and officers in select interest and church groups is a necessary adjunct to acquiring cooperative and work skills in the home. Learn to supervise the various activities of your offspring without living vicariously through them.

6. *Insure your child a kinship network, whether through family or nonfamily relations.* While we all have more living relatives than any other generation since Adam (or Eve), never has the extended biological family had the possibility of being so scattered in space. Sometimes you find it difficult to provide your children with the feeling of "family" that you may have had with grandparents, aunts, uncles, first cousins. Consider the artificial, though not cheap imitation, kinships you may find through the neighborhood families, church associations, or other close friendship sources. Often there are "foster grandparents"

to be found down the street, at church, or where you work, and you will fill a need for them as well as your children.

These "relatives" can provide valuable male models, as crucial in the development of your daughters as in your sons. Male teachers, counselors in scouting, church leaders can provide wholesome life-styles in the absence of a father. Without suitable male figures outside the family, boys appear to be less assertive and more dependent whereas girls are less secure as they approach dating and other heterosexual associations. In today's complex world not even two parents provide enough range of adult models for the socialization of their children. A solo mother just has to be a bit more conscious of this need to provide many positive and varied male, as well as female, adults in the lives of their youngsters.

7. *Keep the communication channels open at all costs*. As the recent slogan goes, children are people, too. Have some time each day when you do not just hear them talking. Listen carefully to *what* they are saying, what they are *not* talking to you about, and what seems to be taking priority in what they talk *to you* about. If there are several youngsters in your family, there should not only be some family talking time, you should try to talk to each one directly and discretely ten or fifteen minutes a day. Sometimes the crises of a young one will prompt you to give all the private talking time to that one.

Oldest and youngest siblings have a way of getting heard. Oldest, because they may have learned to be more aggressive and responsible; youngest, because they often are the more dependent and demanding. It happens in more families than the Waltons on TV that the middle ones get the feeling they're not being heard either by the parent or the other siblings. Watch particularly then for the middle-child syndrome; listen a bit harder perhaps there!

It is pretty difficult not to pull rank when talking and

listening to children. When you're the only adult performing parent roles, don't neglect to convey the feeling that you respect even the youngest's views and ideas . . . even when you must disagree or deny wishes. Assure them that they have the right to disagree with your opinions and decisions, if they do so respectfully and can produce adequate evidence to support their side. Even when you must ultimately enforce your own decision, your refusal to be arbitrary and deaf to their thinking will help maintain open communication.

8. *Teach independence in one's own actions, yet responsiveness to others' needs.* In the growth toward maturity, it is not easy to balance independent decision-making and awareness of need for, as well as the needs of, others. Someone has aptly said that in this celebration of the bicentennial of our independence, what we need is a Declaration of Interdependence! Children need to be given the chance to stand on their own two feet and not be protected from the consequences of their decisions.

The blending of these two traits can often be taught through pets in the home, especially if a child is directly responsible for a particular cat, dog, bird, hamster, or whatever among the family menagerie. Learning stickability in the day by day care for another creature can be a valuable and rewarding experience.

Privacy is one of the essential attributes of even the smallest family unit. Respecting the rights of young and old to be alone, have one's own possessions, and create one's own thoughts is sometimes not easy when an apartment or house seems cramped for its number of family members. A challenge of motherhood is to attempt to provide enough room and psychological space for flexible and uneven growth among the various siblings.

9. *Insulate the discipline and teaching with warmth and honest, open affection.* One of the greatest therapies for

you will be to give abundant evidence of tenderness and love. Funds may be short, there may be no central air and heat systems, cramped quarters may hamper tidiness and order . . . but there is no rationing on joy and companionship. Don't be afraid to express feelings. Children need the assurance of physical affection. Spontaneous hugs and pats can immunize against a host of hang-ups in the growing-up years. One truism they can learn from your example: Knowing love and expressing it does not depend on having a marriage or marital partner. Whether or not they themselves choose to marry, they will know that the married do not have a monopoly on love!

10. *Make no apologies for the moral and spiritual guidelines you provide in every arena of their lives.* Personal integrity of a mother in dealing with the grocer, her job, the relatives, and countless daily encounters provides a constant model for youngsters in honesty on school work, kindness in peer relationships, and dependence on a higher source for moral values. In the absence of a *set* of parents, nothing makes for *double* guidance more than knowing that mom relies on divine assurances and basic religious principles of living.

For a mother to forsake the direct moral and religious instruction of her children to outside teachers and the church or on the grounds that they must have the freedom to search for these verities themselves is to abdicate a parent's most lasting and comprehensive impact. As you teach the facts about sexuality and reproduction, place them in the context of love and marriage as you have known them. As you train them in the use and saving of money through allowances and later their own checking account, stress the stewardship of money and material possessions along with proper use of the body, mind, and talents. They will readily see in your life whether material things are an end in themselves or a means to express care for self, others, and the work of God on earth.

Each of these constitute premiums paid on the life assurance policy that guarantees that your family will not be fractured even when it is incomplete on parents. Particularly "commandments" nine and ten could be responsible for the fact that many children of divorced homes make better marriages than their parents. One parent can be enough to give the emotional, moral, and spiritual context for making a good life. Working for such a homelife can bring to the single mother the reward of knowing that sometimes family can triumph over marriage.

You Don't Have to Do It All Alone

There will be many occasions when you realize two heads would be better than one for finding the answers to some of your problems and needs. Having given a situation an honest try by independently taking inventory and feeling it is too complex for you, seeking counsel is the better part of wisdom. There are several places a mother alone can look for appropriate counsel . . . and make no apologies.

Your banker.—Whether you have been a long and regular customer at your present bank or not, you will usually find a bank officer whose business it is to provide just the kind of counsel you may need on investing or using insurance monies, making a change in kind of residence, getting short, and long-term loans for emergencies. Often this is a free service and is confidential. They are quite accustomed to the many kinds of snarls that can develop after a death or divorce, when there is no will, whether there is insurance or child support, and a variety of other perplexing dilemmas. A few minutes of financial counsel from a discreet outsider can often prevent hours of headaches and months of insecurity following an inexperienced decision.

Your pastor.—While he may not be a trained counselor in nonspiritual matters, your clergyman should certainly be the one for you to seek out in helping you resolve fears and insecurities that have no origin in money matters or other mundane arenas of your life. A talk with him may help you reaffirm your spiritual security and answer the eternal "Why me?" More often than not, he will know about agencies and services in the community to which he can refer you for specialized needs. Because he is generally well-known to these people, a phone call from him may expedite your getting the kind of help you need without delay. Sometimes he may be prompted by your need to have the church promote a colloquim on legal, financial, child-rearing, and other areas important to all widows.

The children's school.—Don't sell your school system short, particularly when your child is having adjustment or academic problems possibly related to the changes that have come in his family. Besides a teacher who often has firsthand, daily exposure to your child's social countenance away from home, there is the principal, the school nurse, or the guidance counselor. Because these are required to have courses dealing with symptomatic signs in child and adolescent behavior, they may be the ones to alert you of a developing problem. If they are not equipped to handle a particular type of problem, they should be able to tell of the nearest child guidance clinics, pediatrician, or child psychologist. The ego-structure of the mature caring mother is not threatened when she must turn elsewhere in helping her child find a normal and suitable pattern of behavior.

Counseling services.—Besides the family lawyer, banker, and pastor, there are often community-supported agencies which assist families through a variety of crises. The Family Service Agency is a national affiliated group which not only offers marital counseling, but also help in parent-child matters. We have already discussed the "Parents without Partners" organization which can supply group therapy and recreation. Doctors can often inform you about free clinics and conferences relative to the health and development of your children. Even if your small community does not provide a variety of these services, there is usually within fifty miles of you a community which can. Look at it as a mark of maturity to know the difference between using someone as a crutch and seeking expert advice in an area in which most mothers, alone or not, could not be expected to have all the answers.

Suggested Supplementary Reading

Baruch, Dorothy. *How to Discipline Your Child* PAP # FL154.

Hallett, Kathryn J. *ATA Primer for the Single Parent*. St. Louis, Mo: Transactional Analyst, 1973.

Hensley, J. Clark. *Help for Single Parents*. Christian Action Com., M. B. C., Jackson, Miss., 1973.

Herzog, Elizabeth & Cecelia E. Sudia. *Boys in Fatherless Families*. Washington, D. C.: Children's Bureau, 1970.

Heatherington, Mavis E. "Girls Without Fathers," *Psychology Today*. (February, 1973) 47-52.

Jones, Eve. *Raising Your Child in a Fatherless Home*. Free Press of Glencoe, 1963.

Kliman, Gilbert. *Psychological Emergencies in Childhood*. Greene & Stratton, 1968.

Neisser, Edith G. *Your Child's Sense of Responsibility*. Public Affairs, Pamphlet # FL254.

7
Steward of My Body

Self-consciousness about one's health and well-being appears so early and universally among humans that it seems almost surely to be an innate trait. In the writing of the ancients about human behavior there was the inextricable blending of the physical, emotional, and spiritual components of life. It was not uncommon for them to mix terminology of this triad as they spoke of the good life. Blood was the heritage and well-spring of life. In the bowels was the seat of the strong feelings and affections of a person. The heart was the source of thought and wisdom, the site of generosity and spiritual understanding. The bones were the structure of an individual, the most lingering remains of a life. The mind was the center of the will, the place where decision making and action began.

There *was* and *is* a wholeness to living. When ancients and moderns have used the greetings *Shalom* and *Salud*, there has been more intended than a mere hello or indifferent "how are you?" There has been a sincere wish for peace and safety, complete good health, and well-being. The genuine desire is for the person to know and have the abundant life.

I believe that a woman, therefore, has a stewardship of health. Being a healthy woman, as anyone knows is more than the absence of disease, disability, or mental anguish.

It is the positive and cheerful outlook on life and the hope for what it can offer in the "now" and in the "later." On the surface that seems a bit more than most of us can manage the majority of our days! Such a view of good health is an ideal. In practical terms, a woman doesn't have to meet life like a Pollyanna or a workhorse, not even with a perfect specimen of body structure to qualify as healthy. For after all, healthy is a relative term. Some of us enter this world with certain biological weaknesses that make us vulnerable in our social and geographical environments, not to mention our life-styles. In such cases, being healthy at best means rising above or coping wisely with an impossible or unchangeable situation. Often it may be only a healthy attitude that helps us enjoy and use life to its fullest within our limitations!

Two young women vividly illustrate my point about the relative nature of good health. I met Jo when I went to my first position following seminary days. She was that rare phenomenon, an ecumenical Bible teacher in the public schools, supported and loved by the four major denominations and the three major faiths in that community. She was bothered by arthritis when I first knew her and it gradually worsened until she was confined to a wheelchair. Her countenance was cheerful even when the pain was at its worst. Her wheelchair seemed more a throne, so regal and impressive was her frail body. Some years later surgery and therapy restored her mobility and miraculously, it seemed, she had renewed vigor and apparent good health. Two years ago I was in her hometown and she called me at the college where I was in a lecture series. While we talked she rejoiced in her restored health, but I drew one inevitable conclusion—her present good spirits and *joie de vie* could not exceed my memory of her fifteen years before when she taught from the wheelchair!

Another vibrant young single woman I came to know in

recent years. Although I was unaware of it, Fran was in her last year of life when I met her during registration as she enrolled for a course of mine. At thirty, she was already blind from diabetes and as frail as a wounded young bird. She taped the lectures and discussions, as well as her tests, making the only A in that course and one of the few in a subsequent upper level course. The family maid drove her to school each day and was her human crutch as she came to class. Her family asserted that those courses were her survival kit that gave her added months of life and happiness. I wonder if the other students and I ever managed to convey to her how much her radiant, pleasant participation in those periods enriched our own mental health and general well-being. She died midway through her third course. Even our grief was a growth experience! She was a living example of unbelievable mental health in a broken, emaciated body.

A woman alone has reason for increased self-consciousness about her total health. When she gives attention to her well-being, aware that often others depend on her good health, this is not synonymous with self-preoccupation. It is the better part of wisdom that she understand and promote the unique blending of her spiritual, biological, and social selves into one healthy personality.

Maintaining the Physical Habitat of Self

The body *is* the dwelling place of the soul and the self. Any astute woman realizes that her body in turn lives in a world that provides both vitalizing and vandalizing forces. She is born with certain sex-linked traits; she is "programmed" for certain potential health-related behaviors. She possesses particular hormones and certain body structure that make her more durable, if not greater in muscular strength, than a man. She is also genetically programmed with certain propensities for "good" or "poor" health because of a unique ancestry which she did not choose for herself! But she will grow up and probably develop some sex-related health behaviors which are determined by the particular life-styles and roles expected in her cultural setting.

It is difficult to know how much of our health is due to our femaleness, how much to our unique inheritance, and how much to our life-style. We are aware that estrogen seems to serve as a protector of our health during forty or more years of our lives, since it retards the accumulation of cholesterol and fat in the blood vessels and wards off the number one killer of men—heart disease. It is equally apparent that some of us probably inherit propensities for diseases such as diabetes, bone deficiencies, or allergies. We are also learning more and more about the biochemical foundations of some types of mental disorders. But it is equally true that centuries of sex-defined roles in western civilization have affected a woman's size and shape, as well as her life expectancy.

Threats to women's health have varied in certain cultural and temporal periods. In America, the death toll from childbearing has diminished and attention now focuses on new dangers like cervical and breast cancer, obesity, hypertension, or accidents. As women move into the labor force in greater numbers and adopt some of the habit-patterns usually associated with working men, there is every reason to expect that they will not only become alert to new opportunities but also prone to additional health risks. Although the death rate from cirrhosis of the liver, lung cancer, or heart attacks has not been as great for women as for men in the past, this may well change. The working woman can expect more ulcers and more tension as her roles expand. Even the suicide pattern has taken a turn toward equalization; whereas, females once primarily "attempted" suicide, they are becoming more "successful."

The stewardship of our bodies requires that we take a close look at some health matters that may not be an exclusive concern for the single woman, but certainly have serious implications as she attempts to establish moral and physical guidelines for good living.

Choosing your doctor.—One of the most important things in your health regimen is finding the best doctor for *you*. You, as a nonmarried woman, need a physician in whom you have confidence and one readily accessible to you. If it seems unwise to have a general or family-type doctor that can treat the general run of ailments for you and any children you may have, then you will want to have an internist or gynecologist that will not be too specialized to treat you occasionally for such nondiscriminating ills as sore throats, earaches, the flu, or measles. Find a doctor with whom you can feel comfortable so that you can communicate about any physical or mental disturbance you feel you have. Remember, doctors have personalities, too, and it is not inevitable that every doctor and patient are meant for each other's well-being!

If you are in a new community or need to change physicians, look in the yellow pages of your phone book for names you can begin to inquire discreetly about among a variety of people whose opinions you trust and respect. Choosing the practitioner to whom you will entrust your (and your family's) well-being is no frivolous shopping venture. Establish contact *before* you are ill and give some thought to your medical history prior to the initial visit. He/she will probably require a number of routine tests and will want to interview you about chronic ailments.

Be sure to inquire about your doctor's policies on house calls. Since you may live alone, you need to understand the procedure for getting emergency appointments, for meeting him at the emergency room in the hospital, and if there is only one hospital he prefers to use. Be candid about regular fees and your insurance protection. Find out if there are any restrictions on getting some temporary or stop-gap medical attention by phone before you are able to secure an appointment.

Illness has a tendency to make the most mature woman react to her doctor in a dependent manner, so plan in advance what you must tell about your symptoms and what questions you need answers for. Since my tendency through the years has been to minimize my pains and to be absentminded about symptoms, I find it helpful to make a list of both my symptoms and my questions. Although my doctor kids me about my "discussion notes," I believe he appreciates it as a logical and time-saving aid.

An ounce of prevention.—There is no better medicine than regular checkups and early detection of symptoms. The average woman today has only about two more disability days per year than a man and this may be largely due to the widespread efforts to educate women about the importance of annual checkups, including a Pap smear. Still, about one third of American women have not had this simple test for uterine cancer and over one half do not repeat it with regularity. A single woman cannot afford this kind of nonchalant attitude about her health. A great host of women who have read about the self-examination for breast lumps do not regularly check themselves. Consequently, tens of thousands of women each year develop cancer and die when simple detection tests and early treatment would have given them very favorable odds for cures. This represents careless stewardship. Pledge yourself to be alert in detecting at least these seven warning signals that call for immediate medical attention:

1. A sore that does not heal
2. Hoarseness or cough that persists

3. Change in a wart or mole
4. Unusual bleeding or discharge
5. Change in bowel or bladder habits
6. Indigestion or difficulty in swallowing
7. A lump or thickening in the breast or elsewhere

The onus of obesity.—Nothing contributes more to the deterioration of a woman's sense of attractiveness or physical well-being than being overweight. While there is much room for variation in a person's conception of "being fat," there are some clearly defined measures of obesity in terms of height, build, and age. Certainly, single women do not have a monopoly on the problem of obesity, but Americans may well have first claim on it as a national malady. A conservative estimate indicates that over 40 million men and women are at least 10 percent overweight. We might accurately say that we need a theology of enough when it comes to food and drink! It almost seems immoral not to get to the causes of overeating when over two million people in this world are malnourished and underweight.

Obesity aggravates many other illnesses you may have such as heart disease, high blood pressure, and atherosclerosis. Diabetes, which is more prevalent among women anyway, is four times more common in overweight diabetics. Thus, obesity is a major factor in other medical problems, but it is also one in itself. One insurance company discovered that the death rate was 147 percent higher than expected for overweight women who were between twenty and sixty-four years of age.

If you are overweight, it is probably due to factors other than heredity or glandular disturbance, such as overeating, imbalanced diets, the need to feed frustrations and loneliness, or irregular meals. If you are more than 10 to 15 percent overweight, you should consult a physician as you would if you were ill. By all means, avoid crash diets. You usually do not become obese overnight, so you should take the excess off gradually with the proper amount of controlled exercise. There are some basic principles to keep in mind as you diet:

1. Keep sufficient protein in your daily diet. The usual for a woman is two ounces of meat, chicken, fish, eggs, or milk per day.
2. Eat at least 1.75 ounces of carbohydrates a day to insure proper bulk and the best utilization of the body's fat.
3. Plan to eat about one third of your diet at breakfast. At first, it may be easier to eat a little bit of your daily diet four or five times daily. This does not mean snacks of forbidden junk foods!
4. If it is difficult to know that you are getting the minimum vitamins needed per day, take a multiple-vitamin capsule.
5. See this regimen not so much as an interim take-off period, but a part of a long-range goal in proper eating.
6. Keep in mind the relationship between caloric intake and the number of calories expended in normal activities. Here are some representative caloric patterns:

Food Intake	Number of Calories	Expended in Exercise per hour
1 T sugar	50	sewing
2 slices bacon	100	rapid typing
2 slices white bread	150	golfing, sweeping
20 large potato chips	200	light gardening
5½-6 ozs. ice cream	250	walking quickly
2 oz. almond chocolate bar	300	easy swimming/bicycling
1 slice apple pie	350	bowling/mowing

At one time dexedrine and other amphetamine drugs

were widely used by women to speed up the weight-loss process, but they can produce many undesirable, even dangerous, side effects such as excitability, insomnia, headaches, high blood pressure. Use them only under the advice and careful supervision of your doctor.

Hypertension.—Women alone are particularly susceptible to this growing worldwide problem of modern living and tension. Some medical authorities are suggesting that there are obvious reasons for women accounting for more and more of the patients who are hospitalized for hypertension and for at least one half of the 200,000 deaths each year due to strokes. They are experiencing stress and even frustration as they expand their roles and as more head up their households. While society may permit us to complain and ventilate more about our anxieties and pressures, thus helping save our lives, you and I may still feel we are unable to channel that tension into enough creative outlets.

Every thinking woman realizes the absurdity of any attempt to live without tension in today's world and with the peculiar pressures of being a parent without a partner or an independent single. But there are ways to avoid unnecessary frustrations and to relieve the unavoidable tensions. Here are the ten commandments for handling tensions, which I reread frequently because I have chosen a busy life-style which breeds tension very easily. Perhaps they will help you.

1. You shall not play Super Self, expecting to accomplish more than is possible or reasonable.
2. You must "talk it out" with someone you trust.
    Verbalizing a problem can be cathartic, as well as prove helpful in getting it in clearer perspective.
3. You shall escape occasionally through realistic and healthful diversion.
    Reading a book, seeing a movie, changing your

scenery can clear your mind and renew your energy for tackling your problem.

4. You can work off your frustration or anger.

    My frustration-energy has pulled many an onion-grass patch out of my carpet grass. In my younger days, on off-days, the Rachmaninoff works got more than their share of my practice time at the piano!

5. You shall "give in" sometimes.

    Stand your ground on principles that are threatened, but yield on trivia or minor quarrels.

6. Tackle only one part of your problem at a time.

    If you are under strain, even a normal load or task can seem overwhelming. Start on the most urgent or top priority aspects of the problem.

7. Do something for someone else.

    Be sure that you don't worry *all* the time about yourself; invest some of your concern in helping someone else.

8. Avoid criticism of others.

    Many needless frustrations are produced by expecting perfection or too much from friends and associates.

9. Make yourself accessible to others.

    Much loneliness and feeling of rejection could be avoided by taking the initiative in being sociable.

10. Schedule your recreation time as carefully as your work.

    Don't feel guilty about playing as easily as you work hard!

Overmedication.—In a conference with nonmarried women recently, I raised the question as to whether women today are seeking in drugs what they may have once found in prayer, church activities, or their husbands' and children's lives. Whatever the answer, it is true that the increased incidence of hypertension in a woman's life these days and the concurrent appeal of the drug stores and pharmaceutical companies for the shopping time of the American woman are probably contributing to her overmedication. American women in days past were concerned with growing their own therapeutic herbs and making the poultices that helped relieve the pains of the family. Now she makes more than her fair share of visits to the doctors and to the local drugstore.

Whether today's woman, single or married, abuses herself through self-diagnosis and patent medicine at treatment or whether doctors are turning more and more to mood-regulating drugs to alleviate the psychosomatic ailments of their women patients, the fact is that between 45 and 50 million women have used such drugs on occasion. A real danger is that a woman can begin to rely on such treatment as a crutch rather than a short-term aid. Women addicts are growing in number, though they still are a decided minority among known addicts.

Alcohol is not a medicine, but an increasing number of women are making it their number one drug problem as it is for the United States as a whole. It is hard to gauge the number of problem drinkers who are women, probably one to every three men—and growing. There are more males in treatment facilities, but there has been an influx of women at Alcoholics Anonymous meetings although there are a great many who are "invisible" problem drinkers. Several facts emerge from the study of women who drink. They are more apt to be problem drinkers if they are married or formerly married. Their drinking is more tied to stress situations (or boredom) than it is for men. More and more, the pressures of professional life or identity crises involving woman's roles outside and inside the home have become a part of this "stress." Women more often than men mix drugs and drinking, a practice that often proves fatal. The drinking of a woman, married or not, is also more apt to remain unexposed; for probably as many as 70 percent of the female alcoholics manage to hide their affliction. For sure, no single woman ever solved her problems or increased her well-being with alcohol!

Nor can one ignore the simple fact of parental influence where drinking is a family experience. Numerous studies could be cited that indicate that not only do more children drink if they come from homes where one or both parents drink, but they drink more frequently. The mother alone carries a heavy responsibility in the area of example, when we read the report from the National Institute on Alcohol Abuse and Alcoholism which indicates that beer is now the favorite beverage among teenagers and that 28 percent of the youths studied had been drunk at least four times during the last year.

Smoking.—Advertising for major tobacco companies has been linking the increased liberation of women with the freedom to smoke. There is no way you can honestly say that a woman who smokes is more brilliant, chic, healthy, or feminine; but cigarette ads are right when they say such women have come a long way . . . to shorter life! The one third of Americans who smoke are writing their own invitations to join the 100,000 who are afflicted with lung cancer, and women are almost equalling men in smoking behavior. More women are smoking, and they are smoking more . . . and earlier.

Lady, if you smoke, you are twice as likely to die of a stroke or heart disease. Know that lung cancer is rising faster than any other female malignancy. As a single woman who needs to work, if you smoke you can expect 15 percent more days at home sick in bed and an additional 20 percent more subnormal productive days. This means you will probably lose three times as many workdays as a nonsmoking woman employee. Let's get even more personal and disturb your ego—you will experience more facial wrinkling, a lower libido, more chances of losing your teeth and having menstrual disturbances!

But don't forget your parental influence if you have had children and are rearing them alone. If you smoked when you carried your babies, you exposed them to risks not only in their embryonic development but created possible long-term effects on their health. Smoke, with or without nicotine, is known to be detrimental to a baby's development. Remember that a youngster is much more apt to smoke if the parent does—and to begin at a younger age. Women who smoke primarily to deter weight gain or to ease their nervousness may be risking double jeopardy—much more serious disease and higher death rate for themselves plus real threats to their children's well-being.

Further Reading on Physical Health

Anders, Sarah F. "A Christian Approach to Women and Health," *Christian Freedom for Women*. Harry Hollis, Compiler. Broadman, 1975.

Benjamin, Annette Frances. *New Facts of Life for Women*. Prentice-Hall, nda.

Boston Womens Health Book Collective. *Our Bodies, Our Selves*. Simon & Schuster, 1973.

Patterson, Robert C., Jr. M.D. *Dr., I'm a Woman!* Nashville: Thomas Nelson, Inc., 1974

Some Public Affairs Pamphlets

Brody, James E. and Richard Engquist. *Women and Smoking* #475.

Irwin, Theodore. *Better Health in Later Years* #446.

Irwin, Theodore. *Watch Your Blood Pressure!* #483.

King, Charles Glen and Britt, George. *Food Hints for Mature People* #336.

Ogg, Elizabeth. *We Can Conquer Uterine Cancer* #432.

Seaver, Jacqueline. *Fads, Myths, Quacks—and Your Health* #415.

8
Being Single *and* of Sound Mind

How does a nonmarried woman separate the building of stable emotions and mature thought processes from the development of a relatively smooth-functioning bodily system? Well, she doesn't . . . any more so than a bachelor or a married woman and man could! The mind and body (and soul) interact. If we worry enough, we are ulcer-prone. When cancer or heart disease strike, there are usually obvious personality changes. When we are spiritually deprived, we may function poorly in mind and body.

Married or single, none of us is perfectly balanced mentally! Mental health is a matter of degree, just as we observed in physical well-being. As we develop during our early years, all parts of our personality do not mature evenly and perfectly. These vulnerable areas of our behavior are the ones in which neuroses or emotional disorders are most likely to appear if they undergo much stress or deprivation. It is both comforting and disturbing for me to realize that I am potentially neurotic, if not already so! Reference has been made already to the research by the sociologist Jessie Bernard in which she discovered the unmarried woman to be generally much better adjusted and more stable mentally than the unmarried man or married woman. Whatever the pressures and stress peculiar to the never-marrieds and formerly marrieds, these women apparently work through them with less loss of mental equilibrium than married women who are experiencing frustrations.

There should be no more disgrace or shame when we become emotionally erratic or mentally ill than when we contract a contagious disease or become physically disabled. Of course, it is far better if those of us who live alone can learn to be objective about our selves to the point that we can admit what appear to be signs of mentally unhealthy behavior. The causes for these changes may not originate in us or be of our making. We already have talked about the fact that we are victims of our society . . . it is a highly competitive, fast-paced, sometimes hostile, and impersonal culture we live in, the more so because we may face it alone. Even when we try to resist the materialistic emphasis, the temptations to be immmoral, the demands of often overly pious people, the unconcern of some churches—we may find ourselves overreacting, hating in return, compromising our standards, feeling unnecessary guilt. And as much as we may hate to acknowledge it, we can seem even to ourselves a little sick, somewhat out-of-balance mentally.

Clues for concern.—What can you look for as signals that you need counsel? Well, for one thing, exaggerated or irrational fears. Everyone has the makings of at least one phobia, but take note when there is no obvious stimulus for your fear or it keeps you from your usual schedule and responsibilities. These questions may serve as a partial barometer of your mental health:

Do your moods shift swiftly and unexplainably? Are you embarrassed because you cry for no apparent reason? Perhaps you find yourself feeling quite antisocial, wanting to sit home night after night even when you have invitations?

Do you fly into uncontrollable fits of anger for minor causes?

Are you so consumed with jealousy or envy over others' good fortune it almost paralyzes your own efforts to achieve?

Do you find yourself daydreaming and fantasizing more and more that your circumstances are much different and your roles much improved?

Have material things become so significant in your life that you would sacrifice almost any principle of honesty and use almost any means to get a bigger house, a promotion at work, a more prestigious car, or a gorgeous and elaborate wardrobe?

Has your vicarious involvement in fiction or television programs become your retreat from the mundaneness of exasperations of your life-style?

Is it easier and easier for you to suspect that others are really out to make things rough for you, that your children do not appreciate you, that your colleagues are imposing on you at the office, that you want no part of God or the church because they haven't seen and met your needs?

Are you depending more and more on pills or alcohol, less and less on the counsel of friends or pastor or expert advisors?

Have you in more than one fleeting moment wondered if no life is better than this one?

If you answer a strong yes to any one of these, then take an immediate first step to get help—do it as quickly and determinedly as if you had just burned your arm.

Seeking help.—See your medical doctor first if there is any possibility your basic problem is physical. Sometimes there are physiological reasons for depression and apathy, so necessary tests should be expedited under his direction.

If you strongly suspect you know the root problem lies in your sex needs, work, loneliness, finances, or religious frustrations, go to the appropriate resource person. Should there be a vagueness or question about the source of your trouble, check your yellow pages in the phone book for a mental health center. There you can find professionals like psychiatric social workers, family counselors, clinical psychologists, and/or psychiatrists. They not only can take you on a short-term or indefinite basis, but they generally have a sliding or graduated fee scale. Best of all, they will keep your confidence perhaps even better than a friend or cohort might.

Some of the most creative and stimulating people I know have included those who have had singular episodes of imbalance or even intermittent bouts with emotional disorders. When I was in graduate school the second go-around, I became aquainted with a sensitive and mercurial young woman who was on the staff in our department. A transplanted Yankee, she was especially gifted with children and she worked with them in a Baptist church near the university campus.

As I came to know her better, I learned she was an only child with a lonely childhood. She confided in me that she had been sexually molested by her doctor when she was in her early teens. Perhaps if hers had been another kind of personality, that trauma would not have left the scars it did. But later when she went on to the seminary and in the following decade or so when both of her parents died, she had to have intermittent therapy in mental hospitals. Yet even so, her Christian faith and her literary gifts have never let her get completely submerged.

Periodically I receive little books of sonnets and haiku full of joy, hope, wonder, and belief in the wholeness of life . . . even from the institution. The example she surely sets for the psychiatric aides and attendants, the creativity that has been diverted from her beloved children's work, the unwavering conviction that God cares for us in all kinds of mental and physical states—there is simply no way I can measure these in her life. Her mental frailty as a woman alone has prohibited her from coping easily with the world "outside" but it has never prevented her from relating to others both "inside" and "outside" her walled-in world through her own media. I would be a lesser person had I never known Anne.

Coping versus copping-out in a crisis.—A single woman does not necessarily have more than her share of crises. For that matter, as we have noted before, the ones she does face are not always unique to her marital status. A crisis is any major transitional experience or disruption in one's normal life patterns. How do you explain women who always seem to bear up well in the presence of personal adversity while others seem paralyzed with terror, panic, or fall apart?

Of course, a crisis need not be a destructive situation; it may be an enriching episode that serves as a catalyst for forming new relationships or life-styles. But as O. S. Marden commented in *Conquest of Worry*, "If your mind is saturated with fear, worry, discouragement, hatred, envy, jealousy, it has no room for the nobler emotions."

One study of human behavior in such critical impacts found that a majority of persons probably do react with minds saturated with negative emotions—about seven out of ten become bewildered and confused; perhaps two stay at least outwardly calm; and one bursts out in anger, revenge, or hysterics. How do you, as a single woman, usually meet these expected or unforeseen episodes of your life? Do you tend to cop out by pretending they do not exist, by ignoring them, or by taking flights into fantasy? Perhaps you jump on your wild horse and ride off in all directions at once, determined to do something, but without due investigation of the situation and deliberate planning.

Loss is a major crisis in the lives of many nonmarried women. It may be the death of a spouse, not getting custody of your children, being divorced or jilted by someone who was an important part of your life and love. Sometimes it concerns situations or *things*, such as being laid off at work, missing a promotion, totaling your car in a wreck, ruining a new or favorite dress. Put the loss in proper perspective. If you were jilted, how much better that it happens now than after marriage! The key is not so much *what* or *whom* you lost, but how much you *think* you lost of yourself and your life plans. Will the course of history be changed by the loss, even the overall meaning of your life? Can you afford to lose your feeling of self-worth and goals along with this blow, no matter how important the thing or person has been to you? Classic examples come to mind of courageous women who answered no.

Fannie Crosby, who lost her physical vision, but refused to give up on her faith and the poetic talent which so wonderfully expressed itself in great hymns. Ann Adams paralyzed with polio and homebound to an iron lung in Jacksonville, Florida, who refused to give up her artistic talent and has built a successful greeting card business, drawing exquisite pictures with a pen held in her teeth.

Disability comes in many forms and often after a loss, as in the lives of Fannie Crosby and Ann Adams. It may follow a mastectomy, a heart attack, or diabetes. It may mean changing the nature of one's work or giving it up entirely. Nell had served in a number of denomination-related positions before she became ill in her early fifties, while serving on a church staff. After surgery for a brain tumor, she was much improved but was told she would be unable to work again because there were remnants of the growth. Accustomed to a busy life, she nevertheless adjusted to the prospects of a slower life-style. Knowing that the growth was of the slow-growing variety, she built a small home near other retired family members in the old home community. Those of us who are occasionally able to visit her and Patches (the cat) in an adjacent state come away with a decided uplift in our spirits, persuaded that anyone with faith like Nell's can lead an inspired life, no matter the circumstances or disability it may be our lot to experience. You may have to forego many of life's pleasures such as tossing a child into the air or playing your favorite sport. It may require getting used to living on a pension or in a convalescent home. When such occur, it is little comfort to know that thousands of others have had your same disability!

If the disability is not yours, but comes to your child or a close relative, your own reaction and outlook may have a significant effect on the victim. With optimism and faith about many options that may still be open to them for a satisfying life, you can help them save themselves from self-pity and resignation and defeat. In the process you will find release from most of your own anxiety and bewilderment about the crisis.

Bad news can be as destructive to sanity and poise as illness or loss. Learning that your son is on drugs when you thought you had such good communication with him; discovering that one of your dearest friends has done a dishonest or immoral thing; getting the word that the person replacing your kind and helpful boss is erratic and demanding; finding out there will be no cost-of-living raise to boost your ailing budget. The list of possible "negative vibrations" is endless. Being mature or of sound mind never has meant that we deal with them stoically. I found that the much-quoted little prayer is more than a clever arrangement of euphemisms; "Lord, please grant me the courage to change the circumstances which can be and should be modified, the grace to accept those which cannot be altered, and the wisdom to know the difference!"

Recently some respected associates seemed to have tended to matters pertaining to my own sphere of work and personnel in an apparently devious manner. The news was not unlike a blow in the stomach, and I felt like washing my hands of the situation and the persons involved. Instead I made myself deal with the people in a straightforward manner, expressing my disappointment and working with them to bring the best possible good out of actions that could not be retracted. There was certainly nothing noble in my attitude or actions. I simply had to determine that it was better to salvage some very good elements in my professional situation rather than to compound the problems with my own retreat or indignation and disappointment. The Chinese were prophetic when they made the written expression of *crisis* with two characters: one means *danger* and the other *opportunity*. A single woman is not judged by the tragedies, the holocausts, the accidents she encounters; rather her measure is in her ability to judge it correctly, seek counsel if need be, explore her options, and learn to live with the most workable solution.

The Matchless Middle Years

The French call the middle years *entre deus ages* (between two ages); among the Spanish they are *de edad madura* (of mature age). Now that I am there, I would call them *sine aequalis* (Latin, without equal)! When I was in my teens and twenties, I thought I would be middle-aged at the critical age of thirty. My dictionary, however, defines the limits as between forty and sixty. How relative age is! I find myself thinking occasionally, "When will I be young enough to retire?"

Sidney Harris called the middle years "that perplexing time of life when we hear two voices calling us, one saying,

'Why not?' and the other, 'Why bother?' " I find myself agreeing with a friend, though, who questioned, "Who on earth said the best years were the teens and twenties . . . I wouldn't be there again for anything. Life may not begin at forty, but it is at its most fulfilling and rewarding!"

There are old wives tales galore to supply those now in their middle years with all sorts of negative expectations about mood changes, uncomfortable bodily changes, and unattractive aging processes. The fact is that none of these is universally true nor do they *have* to be in the vast majority of women. It *can* be two decades of being bored, feeling left at home by the young and put-upon by the elderly. *Or* it can be an exciting time of being at the prime in one's vocation, free and yet secure enough to venture into things you never had the time or money to try before, and (thanks to medical science) optimistic about the next one third of your life that may be the most satisfying and comfortable years of all.

A baby girl is born with all the potential equipment to become a productive and talented woman; every stage she goes through has its special growing (or declining) pains and its own brand of pleasures and assets. The middle years are no different: There are possible menopausal complaints, "empty nest" frustrations, and new pressures; but there is a sense of release from the pressures of youth, marvelous hormonal therapies, and countless innovations in adult leisure activities.

Granted, menopause is a change of physiology that can be dramatic. There are the myriad of complaints associated with it—backaches, irregularities, insomnia, tension, irritability, fatigue, depression, "flushing and freezing" spells, and anxiety. There are specific diseases that correlate with the middle years for women—diabetes, osteoporosis, arthritis. Hopefully, no woman gets them all (unless she talks herself into them or "catches" them from watching the medical shows on television!). Happily, if you make sure that you get a thorough physical examination in your late thirties and continue to have regular checkups through this period, there is little reason for you to experience many of them. As the advertisement on TV says, "She isn't getting older; she's just getting better!"

That is pretty much the thesis of Anne Simon's book, *The New Years—A New Middle Age*, as she points out that we are the first generation of women to be guaranteed another twenty or thirty years, and it is so new that it is practically uncharted. As subsequent generations of women come to this same guarantee of another one third of our lives, society will have worked out all the expected characteristics of this period and absorbed it into a known life-style. It will never again be so exciting, mysterious, unstructured, and *individual* again. Never have there been so many single women in median years of life, and they enjoy a special part of this liberation.

Thoughts About Later Years

"It is not how old you are, but how you are old" (Marie Dressler).

Many social critics have declaimed Americans, particularly womenfolk, for wanting to live longer, but refusing to grow old. I am not at all sure, even with all the writing and talk about the plights of the aged and aging, that we have the neurotic obsessions with looking and acting young as we did even fifteen to twenty years ago. Surely women over sixty-five were among the first to consider facelifts, to don the more comfortable attire of pantsuits, to try for the "natural look in youthful makeup," and to purchase the more economical, "around town" small sportscars. I am persuaded that it was not so much to be something (younger) than what they are, but probably to make more of what they knew themselves to be. No one can fault that attitude toward life.

I think it was the ageless actress Gloria Swanson who commented, "All this talk about age is foolish. Every time I am one year older, everyone else is, too." There are many ways a single woman, or any other for that matter, can look at growing older. At least two are that the later years are a good time to try those things that seemed out of the question in your younger years; or the time when you can rightfully leave off some of the unrewarding, tiresome responsibilities and activities society placed on you before.

For a woman widowed in later years who never worked outside the home because of her family responsibilities, the prospect of training for and going into a later vocation is very challenging. For the single or divorced woman who has had 35 years of continuous work in even a very satisfying vocation, the prospect of a retirement when she can travel, read, visit, putter, or cultivate a hobby or sport beyond anything possible in her working years, sounds like heaven.

If you are among the over 12 million women sixty-five and older, you are more apt to be nonmarried than a senior man. Should you have been postponing marriage until your retirement years when companionship would be particularly welcome, keep in mind the unfavorable odds you will have in searching for such a mate! Seriously, aging has frequently been a more successful venture for us than for them; there are only about 72 men for every 100 women above sixty-five.

There are many myths about the later years of a person's life. The most fallacious is that the psychological, physical, and social characteristics of aging are *all* experienced by *every* older person, man or woman, married or not. Most of us take 25 to 30 years to mature in these areas; most of us will age piecemeal.

Biologically, a woman can separate her aging process into

primary and secondary types. *Primary aging* involves the gradual decline in many types of functioning. You may show it in your stature as you slowly shrink in height or begin to accumulate more bulk through storing up fatty substances. You will probably live longer if you shrink minutely rather than add weight, unless you experience *secondary aging* which can be caused by disease or accidents. A single woman, because she will eat alone more often, should guard against slighting the protein, iron, and calcium in her diet. Most often missing in the diet are milk, fruits, yellow and leafy green vegetables; overly represented are sweets, snacks, and starches. Quite often it is recommended that a senior adult eat four or five smaller meals to enable continual energy output.

In growing older, we may feel that the increased tendency to fatigue indicates we should minimize our exercise when the reverse may be the case. Proper activity can reduce boredom, insomnia, and tedium.

Psychologically, it is a good rule of thumb to remember that when your mind or spirits sag, your body probably will, too. One octogenarian woman professor emeritus, whom I count among my close friends, has such a youthful, inquiring interest in the world beyond her own activities that she appears almost unaware (certainly not bothered by) her loss of hearing or other limitations. The advantage of getting older is that society permits you to order your priorities for expending your energy pretty much as you wish! I think I shall not worry about not having enough energy to continue all of my activities; I shall concentrate in my seventies on giving all of it to my preferred ones! Lord, let me live to enjoy all those books and travel!

A great many women have responded to the tendency of society to "shelve" older people by beginning some new organizations just for themselves. Others prove that they can continue to be a major force in the groups they belong to.

One Sunday during the offertory at church, I counted no fewer than fifty nonmarried older women on my side of the church. When I thought about their contributions to facets of the church program other than the senior adult club and their tithing "mites," I knew that church without them would be not much "church" at all.

Many women dread the thought of spending their last years in a nursing home, and probably from some they may have seen, such a fear is understandable. Barring critical illness or disease, perhaps there are ways that you can forestall that dependency.

1. Consider minimizing your responsibilities of house care by moving from a house to an apartment or condominium where all maintenance is provided.

    In most communities there are very comfortable and cheerful ones for residents who are predominantly older.

2. Make your dwelling less accident-prone.

    Paint steps a bright color and have handrails installed.

    Be sure to have grab-bars and nonskid mats for the bathtub.

    Avoid scatter rugs and use nonskid wax for the floors.

    Increase the wattage of bulbs so that there is ample light.

    Put shields on all heaters and radiators.

    Keep all drawers and doors closed.

3. Take precautions in your own behavior.

    Avoid wearing floppy shoes and trailing garments that catch easily.

    Watch both forward and down as you walk.

    Never leave a room when you have stove burner on.

    Don't smoke in bed or take medications in poorly lit rooms.

    Cross only at intersections and when the signal says *walk*.

4. Remember your weather-conditioning.

    As you grow older, you are most sensitive to heat and

cold.

Have windows and doors weather-stripped.

Avoid getting out in extreme weather.

5. Have regular vision and hearing checkups.

The kind of hearing loss you get with aging causes you to miss background sounds.

Bifocal glasses or cataract lens can cause difficulties in judging distances in the best of lighting.

Don't be embarrassed to get help in dim restaurants, theaters, or churches.

The writer was accurate who declared that "old age is like everything else . . . to make the best of it, you've got to start young." As women alone, it is important to grow old gracefully; it is more important to grow old with *grace*.

Finally

It is absurd, if not impossible, to dissect a single woman's life and wholeness. Yet, we have resorted to that in order to point out that normalcy, fulfillment, or health may vary in the component parts of self and during the stages of a lifetime. It is a major premise of this chapter and indeed of this entire book that the spiritual components of the single life can color appreciably the qualitative aspects of both her mental and physical health. We would venture to maintain even that a sane and vibrant religious perspective will affect our management of the *degree* or quantity of health we possess. Moreover, when we are mindful of the pressures of this last quarter of the twentieth century, it seems that good health can hardly produce the abundant life without full awareness that we are more than psychological, biological female beings.

More Resources on Mental Well-Being

Anders, Sarah F. "A Christian Approach to Women and Health," *Christian Freedom for Women*, Harry Hollis, Compiler. Broadman, 1975.

Benjamin, Annette Frances. *New Facts of Life for Women*. Prentice-Hall, nda.

Gray, Madeline. *The Changing Years*. Doubleday and Co., 1973.

Kaufman, Sherwin A. *The Ageless Woman*. Prentice-Hall.

Retirement Council, Stamford, Conn. *101 Ways to Enjoy Retirement*. New York: American Heritage.

Simon, Anne W. *The New Years - A New Middle Age*. Alfred W. Knopf.

Yates, Martha. *Coping: A Survival Manual for Women Alone*. Spectrum, 1976.

Some Public Affairs Pamphlets

Close, Kathryn. *Getting Ready to Retire* #182.

Irwin, Theodore. *How to Cope with Crises*. #464.

Stern, Edith M. *A Full Life after 65* #347.

Thorman, George and Ogg, Elizabeth. *Toward Mental Health* #120A.

9
Freedom to Become

I am
  my own gardener, cook, mechanic, teacher,
  and "pretty fair country preacher" when I have to be;
  a hostess, often on very short notice,
    and a housekeeper as well.

. . .

I am
  aunt to the MK's
    and "our single missionary" to my peers;
  bookkeeper, lecturer, projector operator,
    translator, social worker, committee chairman,
    and occasional author for the Mission.
I am
  a source of curiosity for African women
    who have never known anything
    but babies and mud huts:
  conscious that African men
    often look on me as an upstart.
I am
  counselor, friend, and educator for youth
    whose search for knowledge often leads them
    away from their Christian commitment;

a shoulder to cry on
 when their hopes for further education
 are thwarted by an alien school system.

. . .

I am
 sometimes lonely, occasionally sick,
  frequently frustrated,
 and often disappointed in myself and others.

. . .

I am
 woman,
 an American,
 a missionary,
 God's child,
 richly blessed.

> CHERYL RAY
> *Missionary in Zambia*

So wrote a single, Protestant woman missionary in Africa, as she faced singleness in an alien culture where unmarried women are at best temporarily widowed and at worst prostitutes—with few, if any, options in between. There are still a great many nonmarried American women who feel like aliens in this, their home culture.

The single women with whom I have talked across the country have contended that regardless of any liabilities and restrictions there might be for singles in today's culture they share a certain degree of freedom. Those who had never married were the most explicit in what this freedom meant to them—a sense of independence in making decisions for which only they were responsible; the opportunity to juggle one's budget and time schedule to enjoy travel; coming and going according to desire; the feeling of not being tied down to one place and one job. But even the formerly married who may have rather heavy responsibilities in the care of dependents and are less able to move the family at will still indicate a sense of satisfaction in being their own boss and using what free time they have in a personally rewarding way.

Honesty demands we recognize that freedom is not the sole possession of either the married or nonmarried. For that matter, in the purest usage of the concept of freedom, no one is completely free regardless of marital status, even as one is seldom wholly restricted or predetermined in her day-to-day living. Oftentimes when one reads through some of the behavioral science books, she may get the impression that these writers are ignoring the possibility of *any* freedom in decision-making or personal events, that we always act within the framework of early childhood conditioning, peer influences, or situational demands. But freedom is a relative experience, in that a person measures her freedom today as greater or less than five years ago and sometimes more or less than that of an acquaintance.

Not only is freedom a relative possession, but it is also a dynamic one. We are not talking now about freedom to *be* but freedom to *become*. When a single woman says she prizes her singleness because she is free to be anything and anywhere she wants to be, it has a smug, static, perhaps even irresponsible ring about it. When she says, however, that she sees her status as an opportunity to grow, to enhance, to improve herself and her world, I say, "Bravo!" In essence, the freedom of the woman alone is measured by three things: what she is free *from*, whether she is free to *be*, and how she is free to *become*.

Freedom from . . .

Freedom is not synoymous with emancipation or libera-

with the most convenient and available person of the opposite sex. Just so, singles often fall into friendship relationships with other unmarried people with whom they have little in common except their singleness. Rather than make a conscious effort to seek out both with whom they can share common interests and backgrounds, single and married companions they contribute to their own frustrations by leaning on the emotional crutch of any alliance that helps them escape loneliness.

One of the oft-mentioned assets many women claim in their single life is the opportunity to have all kinds of interesting friends that cut across the usual boundaries of sex, age, race, marital status, or class. Sometimes the limited leisure time of a working married couple confines them to friends chosen only from business associates, the parents of their children's friends, or the neighborhood. As a single, Protestant, female college professor in my forties, one of my greatest satisfactions has come in the freedom from restraint in choosing my close friends over the years.

As I considered those friendships that have meant the most to me during the past decade, they include such a wide assortment that I might make them uncomfortable if I invited them all to the same occasion in my home! They include a nun with a Ph.D. in clinical psychology, a married man who is a great architect and father, a black woman who cleans my home and shares my books, a sixty-year-old married couple who have much more material worth and compassion than I might hope for, an octogenarian retired literature professor whose most shining example might be her capacity to really listen to people, two former students (one a respected teacher and author in her thirties; the other a very active wife, mother, and community worker in her twenties), an ebullient accountant who lives with and cares for her parents, and the foster mother of my two godchildren who has combined the best of being single and being a "mama." And that is wealth!

Loneliness.—This complex, derivative emotion was not invented by and for the unmarried! While all persons are not equally prone to loneliness, it is no respector of status, sex, or the usual social separators. More often than not, it clearly points up the universal need we all have for other human beings in that it usually presents its depressive response in the absence or loss of a particular human relationship. This basic need or drive can be as general and as specific as hunger or thirst. We can be hungry in general for almost any food that is a part of our cultural diet, or we can crave strawberry shortcake in particular. We can want to be at a faculty gathering or church service to share with our associates in general, and we can yearn to see a parent we haven't been able to visit in six months or to be able to chat again with a close friend who died a few years ago.

There are many aspects to the feeling. An eight-year-old left with a new babysitter while the parents go to the theater and dinner feels loneliness in a different manner than the fifty-year-old widower who has just lost his wife of 26 years or the forty-four-year-old mother whose last child just left home for college. Loneliness can be precipitated by external factors such as a fourteen-year-old girl feels when her father is transferred to another city by his company and she must leave all of her friends. But it is also an internal, permeating attitude when an eighty-three-year-old widow in a nursing home is aware that every day's obituary carries the names of her friends, and she feels her children in another state no longer care about her enough to visit often.

Any adjusted, contented person can assure you that aloneness is a different experience from loneliness. Aloneness is self-privacy that the strong, the mature, the sociable, the leaders, the helpers, and the busy all cherish; it is recreative and restorative. But loneliness—it can be debilitating mentally and physically. The woman alone who does not cope positively with protracted loneliness discovers she is anxious, can not sleep well, loses weight, and may have intermittent periods of lethargy, crying, and restlessness.

Women who live alone or perhaps with their children at a distance from friends and relatives, may brood over a man's advantage in initiating relationships and social events in our society. Some of you may feel hesitant to go places alone, unescorted—particularly if you grew up in a family that stressed chaperonage for females at all ages. Nevertheless, we *are* living in a new social era; so take charge of your situation and get freedom *from*. Find yourself at least one absorbing and satisfying hobby, preferably one that can be shared through some social group. Then, don't wait to be included in a social occasion—invite some old and some new acquaintances to a dessert party, a covered-dish dinner, or an after-theater coffee. Determine that you *will* accept or give at least one social invitation each week.

Holidays and special occasions can be the most isolating times because they are so often "family times." Plan especially for these occasions. If it is not a time when you can be with some of your family or friends, plan a sightseeing trip somewhere you often have wanted to go. Times of illness and convalescence also may make you vulnerable to loneliness. As you begin to feel stronger, treat yourself to a long-distance call to one of your favorite people with whom you have not talked in a long time or read a particularly good and humorous book.

You can't ignore loneliness, but you can make people a genuine object of interest. Make a point of speaking to new and stimulating people you have been attracted to at professional, church, or social gatherings. Really *hear* them when they talk to you. Make sincere interest a habit and before long, you will be able to choose the ones you will reserve for the deepest relationships from an assorted group of acquaintances. Perhaps then the closest thing to a problem may be finding that coveted time for aloneness!

Freedom to Be

More than once we have stressed that a single woman, as much or more than any person, needs to reexamine and appreciate her worth. It is not enough that we free ourselves *from* certain undesirable attitudes and alliances although we truly do not want to be like Paul Tournier's friend whom he quotes in *The Person Reborn*, "I am like Lot's wife . . . my life is petrified because I keep looking back." Having freedom *from* is not enough to guarantee that we will live abundantly in the present, accepting and even liking ourselves.

There is no way that you and I can have an accurate perception of our world and our place in it until we can honestly look at ourselves and say without conceit, this is a person I *love*. Some things I do not particularly *like*, indeed I may positively despise about myself, nevertheless I must love *me*. How else can I respond to the command to love my God with my whole being and others (some I even have difficulty liking) with the same quality of love as I have for myself? Being single, divorced, separated, or bereaved doesn't enter the matter of affirmation at all. Nor have any bearing on my state of loveableness. Dag Hammarskjöld, the Swedish bachelor who became Secretary-General of the United Nations in the late 1950's, wrote in his *Markings*: "To be free, to be able to stand up and leave everything behind—without looking back. To say Yes . . . To say Yes to life is at one and the same time to say Yes to oneself."

Freedom to be for the woman alone consists also of the freedom to be open with others. I suppose that this comes really only after you (probably like Narcissus the Greek lad) come to love yourself not because you are so beautiful, but because you can accept even your ugliness. And only after you can judge your at-homeness and contentment without comparison to others' circumstances, do you come to the point where you are free to take off your masks around others you work and associate with. Then, and only then, will you lose the need to act simply in response to others' behavior toward you. You, as a single woman, are comfortable in being yourself in every kind of social situation. Such is maturity.

Freedom to Grow

Paul Klee proclaimed, "Becoming is superior to being." The final measure of Christian freedom *is* whether one grows. As already observed, the responsible, mature freedom of any person can never be static. Like the apostle, the single says, "My friends, I am still not all that I should and can be, but I am bringing all my energies to focus on this one thing; I am leaving the past behind and looking forward to what lies ahead, I want to reach out and grasp the goal" (Phil. 3:13-14, author's paraphrase). Thank God you are made to grow!

Stretching the mind.—Is your mind all kinked up with worry about today's problems and tomorrow's work? Has everything you have read lately seemed related to your job or filling out your income tax? As a single woman, you want to be truly a free and growing mind, but you know that a really literate person exercises that mind with more than the television tube or the grocery list.

What *was* the last book you read? If you really want to stretch your mind, start by rereading some of the classics that you once read simply because some teacher required it. Try some stimulating biographies, not just about the greats of the past like Helen Keller, Susan B. Anthony, Bill Wallace, or Albert Schweitzer. Read about some controversial people, past and living, such as Aaron Burr, Angela

Davis, or Martin Luther King, Jr. A moving story of a contemporary doctor, Bob Hingson, is *Operation Brother's Brother*. Another is Corrie ten Boom's *Hiding Place*. Try fiction from among the favorites by Charles Dickens to some of the contemporary writers as Shirley Grau or Walker Percy. You do not live alone when you read lively provocative fiction and biography.

Read for self-improvement. Over the years I have particularly been helped by Paul Tournier's *The Meaning of Persons*; John Killinger's *For God's Sake, Be Human*; C. S. Lewis' *The Four Loves*; Roy A. Burkhart's *The Person You Can Be*. But there are more, many more. You don't have to buy books, your taxes have already built a public library, so consider your lending card a necessity rather than a luxury. Pledge yourself to enlarge your vocabulary; add at least three new words to your speaking vocabulary from every book you read.

Spending your talents.—If freedom is more than being husbandless, with or without children, then growth is more than soaking up knowledge, attending lyceums, making the most of educational television programs—it is searching out one's special gifts and capacities, exercising and training them, and then investing them in worthwhile experiences.

I remember a paper Bette wrote the beginning of her senior year in The Family course. For five years after college, she said, she was going to do her thing, get a good social work position, buy a sports car, enjoy the nifty clothes that were too much for a collegiate budget, have a swinging apartment, and TRAVEL to rid herself of provincialism! ALL of this must have been a passing freedom flight into fantasy for it certainly belied the pious, strict upbringing she had had and the solid, steady countenance she had maintained in my association with her. Now a decade later, I have beheld her sense of fulfillment as she served in the Teacher Corps in the Appalachian poverty belt for modest salary and postponed a family of her own while molding and motivating youngsters in that target deprivation area along the eastern seaboard. If and when she leaves the single life for a home and family of her own, I suspect there will be only slight twinges of regret, if that, for the gay and carefree single life that might have been.

A gift or talent is something vested in us, through no striving or appealing of our own. There is no such thing as a talentless single, only a blind and faithless self who will not heed the writer of Romans when he says, "Be honest in your estimate of yourself, measuring your value" (12:3, TLB). *

It is a gift if you are born beautiful in countenance and figure. But many of us must be satisfied with cultivating the latent gift of attractiveness! It is no sin to draw out our natural good features by clothes, cosmetics, and accessories that are becoming. I suspect it may be as much a sin not to enhance our strong physical assets though they seem few in number, as it is a sin to neglect the inner beauty.

Find your functional gifts, also. Perhaps you have drifted away from the piano or guitar, your painting, a sport such as tennis or golf, the knack for sewing or handicraft. Determine today to select at least two of your past or present aptitudes in different areas and concentrate on retraining and using these interests, not just for your own enrichment but to share with friends. Everyone needs to have two quite different pastime interests, because leisure needs vary greatly according to your work day, your energy level, and your need to be with other folks.

Some gifts you may be inclined to overlook are those in your personality. A very dear single friend of mine, ever so different from this more reserved and private writer, completely fills any room she enters with goodwill and generosity. Nursing home managers could well employ her just to pass through twenty minutes a day and invest her glow and joy of living! She comes as near literally giving the coat off

---

* From *The Living Bible, Paraphrased* (Wheaton: Tyndale House Publishers, (1971). Used by permission.

her back and going the second mile for people in need as anyone I have known. For a fact, she has borrowed money to help someone in an emergency for she says, "My credit rating is usually better than theirs!"

Another single thirtyish friend of mine is handier and more agile with tools than most men I know for she is a skilled artist in crafts and mobiles. One of her greatest joys and least publicized gifts is visiting regularly some of the older pensioned widows in her community taking care of loose doorknobs, doing minor carpentering repairs, gluing this or that, hanging pictures, painting here and there. I have often bemusedly fantasized all of these little white-haired ladies rising up to call her blessed when she joins them finally in the happy hereafter!

Single women playing their multitudinous and often androgynous roles may become so weary of all the necessary doings that they neglect their most valuable resource—their "self." For many years I have talked about and seriously tried to schedule my "Be kind to Sarah Frances" days, not to orgy in some ecstasy of self-preoccupation, but rather to allow myself some growing room by just riding a bike through the woods on a fall day, spending all Saturday in my pajamas, walking barefoot mentally through a wide assortment of reading materials, designing and making a dress like one I saw that was far beyond my professor's budget, playing and singing with the kind of skill I could hardly expect many others to appreciate!

Soaring of the soul.—Some of those days were aimed at letting my soul catch up with my body. These are the days when I understand what Paul meant, "I do not intend to imply that I am perfect. I haven't learned all that I should yet, but I want to keep expanding myself for that day when I will finally be all that Christ saved me to be and to do" (Phil. 3:12, author's paraphrase).

Nor do I intend to imply that we should save our tired

days to *be* spiritual and to *grow* spiritually! But you must admit, however, that there are Sundays when the accumulated workweek of your single life make it impossible for your church attendance to do much for your influence, much less permit your soul to soar. Improvement in appearance, professionally, mentally, or in talent is not the whole picture. There must be time for more than spiritual first aid. When you reserve only the last few minutes of a fatiguing day for devotional time or only crisis times for searching through prayer, that is about all you get—first aid.

Nothing can take the place of communal worship in enlarging your spiritual horizons. Remember churches and church programs have "personalities" or characters, not unlike individuals. If you are not experiencing the feeling of unity or the challenge of service in your church, take inventory of your situation. Perhaps there is another of like faith that will speak to your needs. However, if you find a church fellowship that speaks only to *your* needs and you can find no part of its program in which to contribute your specific ability in meeting others' needs, be assured you will not grow there. You will soon lose your sense of well-being if you merely soak up the spiritual without giving and participating yourself. No church will intentionally shut a single out of any of its programs. Not even family events, for the church *is* a family to all.

Some of the most effective programs in the community or the church have been begun by those who felt there was a vacuum in their own lives. This has certainly been true among the unmarrieds, as well as parents without partners. Start with an informal fellowship and move into plans for a Bible class in your church or a social organization that is open to all singles, churched or unchurched, in the community. Expect to invest a great deal of work . . . and do not be discouraged by slow beginnings. Sometimes you have to move person by person in order to interest such a diverse group. If your church has a staff member in charge of the educational or activities programs, this person can offer many practical suggestions and help.

Churches may offer spiritual and pragmatic support simultaneously through members who are doctors, lawyers, and professional counselors. These can provide occasional or continuing "Big Brother" seminars for nonmarried women who are confused by insurance, legal contracts, business details and personal/spiritual dilemmas. Such resource people would not be forfeiting a fee by leading such discussions, but may establish relationships of confidence that will encourage the woman alone to consult him when she reaches a crisis. Sessions could also deal with such matters as security, health matters, investments, or how to deal with unscrupulous businessmen as well as theological issues.

There are also special volunteer ministries that nonmarried women will excel in. Above average in education often, some might be trained and used for counseling with adolescent girls on matters of abortion and illegitimacy. Find the most suitable time—it may well be other than Sunday. Women, regardless of marital status, have always constituted a substantial part of church memberships. They also have played significant roles in missions, visitation, and music, as well as many types of teaching situations. To turn a well-known phrase, most single women ask not what the church can do *for* them, but what useful roles they can perform in *their* church.

The church cannot overlook numerous single and formerly married women who give selflessly to church vocations. While I do admit that sometimes even the church has discriminated against this work force in salary and benefits, I cannot agree with Margaret Mead when she wrote in Beverly Cassara's book on the changing image of American women, "Society holds so low an opinion of women who work seriously for the church, either professionally or otherwise, that it often assumes that such women are either of low mentality or victims of neuroses" (1962, p. 12).[1] While there are proportionately few women in the ministry, they are involved in a wide variety of religious vocations, such as social work, education, medicine, music, missions, or counseling. Religion in America would have been sorely lacking and inept without the contributions of not just married women but those who were "married" to their religious calling.

Sifting the social.—The forty-hour workweek is an illusion to most single women. There are many after-job duties to be tackled by the single head of a household that make "leisure" hours a misnomer. Trite and obvious as it might sound, all work and no social activities add up to tension and dullness for Single Susan. Having led retreat sessions and various seminars for both married and singles groups, I know that providing well for leisure hours is a problem for many persons.

Start with a look at your attitude. Are you a workaholic, not happy unless you bring work home? Is your work an excuse so you won't have to deal with the question of friends and social engagements? I have known women who met their entire life like a workhorse, tensing every muscle and making every activity a chore. Americans have even been accused of working at their play. Many people return from vacation or an evening with their hobby or sport so fatigued and depleted, they need bedrest!

The happy, fulfilled life is a well-rounded one. If you spend more than forty-five to fifty hours on your work or in your business, take a look to see if you are using your time

---

[1] Beverly Benner Cassera, (ed) *American Women: The Changing Image* (Boston: Beacon Press, 1962), p. 12.

wisely. If your day is so full of needless phone calls, trivial errands, or the poor work habits of your associates that you inevitably take work home from the office or lab, talk with your employer about better time budgets for you and the entire working situation.

As already suggested, every single woman needs two options at least for leisure time in order to find relaxation from special kinds of working days. There should be a balance between the very active and the sedentary, the creative and the passive interests. Avoid having more than one leisure activity that requires expensive materials, equipment, or fees. Despite what we sometimes feel, there are rewarding *and* inexpensive pasttimes.

If you have children, some of your free time should be family experience, such as trips to the park, lake, museum, or zoo. Occasionally, you will be a spectator for your child's participation in sports, performances, and other school events. Never, never assume that all of your leisure time and interest must be directed toward the children's or family events. A personal social life and participation in organizations with your peer group constitute a healthy and satisfying necessity.

The art of conversation and visiting seems to be a vanishing one. Schedule a visit to the homes of relatives or friends at least once a month. Don't assume because your friends are married that they have no desire to spend time with you in their home or attending social events. If they truly are your friends and find you delightful and stimulating company, your marital status is inconsequential.

Maybe you need to take a good look at your brand of friendship. On a scale of one to ten, would you rate nearer "three" or "eight"? Do you use the same rating scale for yourself as you do for others? Try these criteria on yourself—the ten commandments of being a friend:

1. **A friend accepts.** Accept is stronger affirmation than tolerate which often carries a negative tinge to it, as though one merely endures or suffers through the differences of another person. The mature woman knows that humanness is a unique blending of positive and negative traits. She finds the differences stimulating. Pablo Casals was correct when he observed, "The main thing in life is not to be afraid to be human."
2. **A friend is consistent.** Even with allowances for shifts in moods, there is steadfastness in the relationship. Being a friend is an active, continual, sure experience.
3. **A friend is loyal.** This assumes that you are with me not only in times of joy, but also in stressful, sorrowful, and plateau experiences of life. Even when I disagree with you in belief or action, I am loyal in granting you the right to decide, sometimes to be right and other times wrong.
4. **A friend loves.** We experience *agape*, for we love when we do not always like or approve or get. Ours is a reciprocal relationship, not measured in percentage distributions. We do not care for each other *in spite* of our differences or *because* of them, but rather *through* them. We make our uniqueness work *for* our relationship. As e. e. cummings the poet expressed it, "Unless you love someone, nothing else makes any sense."
5. **A friend is honest.** We can partially agree with Edward F. Benson's observation, "How desperately difficult it is to be honest with oneself. It is much easier to be honest with other people." The greatest skill, perhaps, in friendship is to be able to discern between brutal truth and tactful, helpful truthfulness. I must be as open as our relationship can bear; I would hope that I can accept such honesty from my friends. Respect me enough that you do not have to lie to me or flatter me

when I use poor judgement or do wrong.
6. **A friend can listen.** So few people really *hear* you in most social conversation. How fortunate if friendship can provide you with a sympathetic and caring audience especially in problem areas you would expect to share with a husband if you were married. Such a person understands that such listening does not always require advice or judgment. Just the process of talking to a caring person often is enough to sort things out for oneself logically enough to know the wise decision or action to take. Listening is an art I want to develop.
7. **A friend is not a burden-tramp.** As a friend I must not exploit our relationship by coming to you and parking my troubles or upsets because you have a willing ear and heart. As a woman alone, I must be mature enough to handle the bulk of my crises alone. I cannot abuse a friend's good nature by transferring the troublesome trivia and then going off carefree.
8. **A friend can keep confidences.** Occasionally well-meaning friends become so concerned about your crises or dilemmas that when you confide in them they immediately go out to do battle for your cause or to right the wrongs done to you. Just because I share an event or experience with a close friend does not mean that I want anything more than passive involvement or compassionate listening. A conscientious friend can readily say, "My lips are sealed. You can trust my discretion."
9. **A friend complements me.** Imperfect as I am, I rely on my friends to fill out the deficiencies in my personality and abilities. You help me to be "whole" because you possess many traits that I admire. When we are together, we "click," for we work and play smoothly as a team. Each of my friends does something unique for me; I need them all for the total occasions of my life.

10. **A friend helps me grow.** Many times the traits I admire in my friend cause me to stretch myself in order to absorb these qualities into my own life-style. The joy of friendship is the inspiration and challenge to be all my potential will permit. As the writer said, "I love you for helping me build from the timber of my life not a tavern but a temple."

History may someday indicate that America is indebted to nonmarried women. We are surely indebted to America for the social climate that permits us to grow freely in most directions. We are obliged to keep alive our assets in responsible freedom, adventure, and service. Count your blessings!

More About Personal Growth

Anderson, Wayne J. *Alone but Not Lonely.* Deseret Book, 1973.
Bontrager, Frances. *Church and the Single Person.* Herald Press, 1969.
Burkhart, Roy A. *The Person You Can Be.* Harper & Row, 1962.
Edwards, Marie & Eleanor Hoover. *The Challenge of Being Single.* J. P. Tarcher, 1974.
Jepson, Sarah. *For the Love of Singles.* Creation House, 1970.
Killinger, John. *For God's Sake, Be Human.* Nord, 1970.
Lawson, Linda. *Life As a Single Adult.* Convention Press, 1975.
Lewis, C. S. *The Four Loves.* Harcourt, Brace, 1960.
Marshall, Catherine. *To Live Again.* McGraw-Hill, 1957.
Scanzoni, Letha and Hardesty, Nancy. *All We're Meant to Be.* Word Books, 1974.
Tournier, Paul. *The Meaning of Persons.* Harper & Row, 1957.
Tournier, Paul. *The Person Reborn.* Harper & Row, 1966.
Tournier, Paul. *The Whole Person in a Broken World.* Harper & Row, 1964.

10
A Woman's Privilege: To Change Her Status

> Love always looks for love again,
> If ever single, it is twin,
> And till it finds counterpart,
> It bears about an aching heart.
>
> R. H. Stoddard

No one can dispute that American marital life-styles are dynamic and varied. Many times in this book, we have stressed that singles are as myriad in type and behavior as are married people. Like marrieds, singles also have the privilege of changing their minds . . . and often this means changing their marital status. Last year alone, over one million married women "changed their minds" (or their husbands did!) and became single again. That did not mean necessarily that they changed their minds about the institution of marriage, only about their marriage partner. Well over twice as many single and formerly married women changed their minds about the single life and took the big step into matrimony. That means over three million women every year are going through some transition in their marital status, and this does not even include the several million who become widowed or separated during a year's time.

There are nine kinds of marriage that involve nonmarried women. Consider the possibilities of the single (S), divorced (D), or widowed (W) woman (W) or man (M):

SW — SM*	DW — SM***	WW — SM
SW — WM	DW — WM	WW — WM
SW — DM****	DW — DM**	WW — DM

The most numerous type of marriage in America is still between two never-married (SW — SM*) and fairly young people (23.1, 21.1). But single women do opt for marriage in later years and increasing numbers of divorced or widowed women are trying marriage for the second and third times. (The asterisks indicate 1st, 2nd, 3rd, 4th frequency ranks in kinds of marriage). While the marriage rate has been holding relatively constant then, the remarriage rate has been climbing steadily and rapidly. We can expect a growing number of late marriages and also reconstituted marriages. It seems that even the most determined single woman, the most burned divorcee, and the most grieved widow can—and do—change their minds!

The late marriage: "I Believe I'll Try It After All"

The older she gets, the less likely a single woman will marry. Both widows and divorcees outnumber her at the altar after thirty years of age. Singles make up only about 16 percent of the women who get married at forty. Numerous studies, however, indicate that she will be more confident, poised, and well-adjusted for marriage than younger or once-married brides. Although she is not as apt to be chosen as a marriage partner by older men, she will generally be a more stable spouse even without previous experience. A man who thinks any experience in marriage (whether good, indifferent, or miserable) is better than no experience shows his own naivete, if not his poor judgment! Experience may be a *dear* teacher, but it may only teach you by negative example. Former marriages may show you what you do not want to repeat, not necessarily what a good marriage is all about.

A single woman who decides after the first bloom of youth to marry still has the same three options—a bachelor, divorced, or widowed man. But she can probably expect him to be a somewhat older man whose former marriage ended less than three years ago. There is a strong likelihood that she will become a stepmother, but her adjustment to the children will be less traumatic because they will probably be older and not live with her and their father. If the husband is divorced, the mother will probably have custody, and they will be children or teenagers, for the father will be in his middle-to-late thirties. But if he is widowed, he is likely to be in his fifties, and the children will probably be away in college or beginning to marry themselves.

Why do single women delay marriage until they are middle-aged? As we have discussed earlier, very seldom will it be due to unattractiveness, physical handicaps, or lack of opportunities. Perhaps the ones you know something about have enjoyed the best of singleness—a good career, traveling, considerable freedom, the incentive for extensive education. Such a woman has not only been single, she has been single-minded! She may wake up one day and discover that some relationship she has been particularly enjoying with a colleague is more than platonic. Now she is confident and relaxed enough in a very fulfilling life to include another time-consuming component of the good life—a companionable and challenging marriage! Perhaps it wasn't sought or prayed for, it is a serendipitous surprise and benefit of the good life.

As I thought about my own never married friends, at least six came to mind readily who had married for the first time in their forties. Two of them even had children during this last decade of child-bearing! As one talked to me recently about this book, she only half-jokingly remarked to me, "Now, Sarah, if you include me in some chapter, be sure to make it clear that I had taken time for all the rich living of singleness before I took the big step. . . . I had gotten two master's degrees, cared for my mother until she died, lived abroad a year, and traveled extensively, plus cultivated a host of friends. I had deliberated at length about marriage, had a tubal ligation, planned on several more years in my profession—and finally took the leap of faith for the last one third of my years to be spent as a wife-companion." There was no doubt in my mind that it had been a big decision for her to make; she had carefully weighed the pros and cons because she figured there were still more than twenty years ahead of married living!

One said she finally tired of making all of the major decisions alone—such as servicing the car, tending the lawn, calling the plumber, and determining whether Red China should have been admitted to the United Nations! Joke as they might about their reasons, these mature single women have made surprisingly good marriages, proving very flexible and adjustable to the couple-way of doing things. One thing I invariably note about these later marriages is that the mates seldom suffocate each other. While they value their companionship and shared activities, they maintain privacy, independence, and "room to breath" for themselves.

Marriage Recycling: The Restructured Family

Following Divorce.—One sociologist has commented that there are now in American society more people experiencing plural marriages than in some societies that called themselves polygynous. Of course among our forebears, remarriage followed very quickly after the death of a spouse. The agrarian economy demanded teamwork and fertility; remarriage was not only a sacred but an economic necessity. But today remarriage more frequently follows divorce than death. Since the 1960's, the trend has been toward one out of every four marriages being a remarriage. There are over 200,000 couples, in which at least one of the pair has been married three or more times! Three fourths of the remarriages in the United States have involved divorced persons and the remaining one fourth were widowed. The restructured marriage of the divorced occurs after a shorter interval of nonmarriage also—a typical divorced person waits less than three years, whereas the typical bereaved spouse waits over four years to remarry.

Once more with feeling.—Approximately 400 thousand marriages per year involve divorced persons. If women are under twenty-five years of age when they divorce, 90 percent will remarry. At any age the case of the remarrying divorcee is clearly one of hope triumphing over experience. Whether one assumes, shares, or projects the blame for the mistakes made in the first union, hope does seem to spring eternal in the breast because the odds are seen as much more favorable with a new partner. As we will see, this optimism may or may not be justified. Most divorcees will wait less than five years to remarry after a first marriage which lasted approximately six years, so the second wedding occurs by her middle thirties. Of the women who marry at forty, at least 65 percent will be divorcees. The longer the first marriage lasted, the longer will usually be the interval before remarriage.

Neither the hope nor the frequency indicate the barriers or hindrances that the church or society may place in the way of such marriages. Some states have a waiting period following divorce before remarriage can occur. The Catholic Church still holds a very conservative view on the sanctity of marriage and the banning of remarriage while a former spouse is alive. Some Protestants are equally restrictive and teach that such marriages—even when they involve the so-called innocent party of a divorce due to adultery—should be entered cautiously and with the permission of the church. More liberal denominations feel that marriage and divorce are private and civil matters, to be considered as religious matters apart from the church. This view may hold that many church weddings were not necessarily sanctioned by God and hence when love is gone it is adulterous and sinful to continue the marriage.

For any woman who is sincerely persuaded that marriage is a divine as well as a human commitment, there will be the need to resolve these questions and usually with the benefit of counsel from a trusted and wise pastor. Moreover, it is not enough for the woman to be assured that she is not violating her religious principles; the husband-to-be must share the conviction that this will be a "right" relationship theologically and spiritually.

If you are divorced and would like to remarry, you have theoretically the same options as a single woman—to marry a bachelor, a widow, or another divorced person. Yet the most frequent choice will be the selection of a man who is divorced. Once-marrieds tend to gravitate toward each other, but the formerly married will have patterns of courtship and engagement which are quite different from the never-marrieds. The period of dating and courtship tends to be shorter and more informal. Only about one half will announce their engagements. Far fewer, proportionately, will have an engagement ring, prenuptial showers, and a formal wedding. Judson and Mary Landis found in their research that a majority of these remarrying still had parental approval (over three fourths), but not as much so as the singles (90 percent). Fewer go on wedding trips and have difficulty in sex adjustment in the early stages of their marriage. This may be due to the fact that a surprisingly large number admitted to premarital sex (about 75 percent), as compared with those who were first-marrieds (35 percent).

Many premarital considerations are unique to the couple

who are trying marriage again, consequently most of them frankly express more doubts beforehand. There are the very practical matters such as a new will, the possible adoption of the other spouse's children, and whose residence they will live in. Many do not feel that the Kennedy-Onassis marriage contract should be peculiar to the wealthy and famous; so they draw up legal agreements about matters which involve work and house responsibilities, child care, inheritance, properties, and even burial places. There are also other very serious matters which cannot be contracted, such as feelings toward stepchildren and toward having more children, but which must be settled nonetheless.

If you are remarrying, perhaps you should examine your motives even more carefully than if it were the first time around. Sometimes there can be very immature reasons for rushing headlong into a second marriage—a desire to squelch leftover love feelings for the first husband, to get revenge because he married right away, the need to get a father and supporter for children, the panic to find a companion of almost any kind to ease the loneliness and guilt, the craving to show the world and your friends that after all you are not so unlovable. The reason most given? LOVE! But if any of these factors should be a major push, can you afford to stack the odds against your success so much? My grandfather used to say, "Even a mule doesn't step in the same hole twice!" But a great many formerly married people repeat their same mistakes in their next marital relationship.

A number of studies of remarried persons indicate that the divorcee who attempts a second marriage is as well-adjusted as most married women the first go-around, but not so the divorced and remarried man. Still, it takes two to tango, as the saying goes; and when one partner is poorly adjusted or unhappy, the marriage does not have optimum chances for success.

The second time around.—Of about eleven million restructured families, it has been estimated that about 10,000 involve the remarriage of the same two spouses! Now the reasons for these "second time around" weddings can be very interesting. Perhaps the divorce grew out of an explosive rift which both regretted and then came to see how much they really loved each other. Some of these couples ignore the months or years apart and count anniversaries from the first wedding. Some loved each other, drifted apart in different interests, failed to work hard enough to prevent the divorce—then absence makes them aware of their real need and dependence on each other and each resolves to accommodate more the second time. Still others want to prove the first time was not really a mistake—they feel guilty or think they are hurting the children. If the reconciliation doesn't work out, these are likely to say, "Well, no one can say I didn't give it another try."

Perhaps you are aware of some marriages that have broken up and the second try for the couple followed an interim when one or both were married to another partner. This really becomes a complicated situation and one that sounds like children's relationships more than those of mature adults. Not only do you have a responsibility for hurting each other, now you have the additional remorse for having interrupted and pained someone else's life as well. This type of remarriage seldom follows a regular dating or courtship period, and the marriage is quiet, at a civil office or the pastor's study.

Remarriage of the widow.—Over 100,000 widows marry each year. They usually wait almost five years after the death of their husbands and are in their early fifties. If they are mothers, they are probably by this time also grandmothers. Through their bereavement, they have had the social support of sympathizing relatives and friends; and assuming their first marriage was reasonably happy, they are basically optimistic about remarriage. Indeed, if their marriage lasted twenty to twenty-five years they may miss the life-style of marriage tremendously and never quite adjust to living alone or with their children.

There is always the tendency to idealize a loved one who is deceased. Often you are loathe to speak of his faults or your bad experiences with him to those who express sympathy for you; so the longer you sweep aside the negative memories the more inclined you are to exalt his personality and qualities. Consequently, if a widow does not remarry soon it may become more and more difficult for any man to measure up to (if not to match) the image of the former mate. Constant comparisons between the living and the dead, in courtship or marriage, can wreck a potentially good relationship.

Often the adjustments to a new marriage will not be as dramatic and demanding for the widow as for either the remarrying divorcee or single woman. Nevertheless, there will be numerous business and financial matters that need to be cared for in the prewedding period. Often these couples are more financially secure and can manage a lengthy wedding trip. A seventy-year-old, twice-widowed woman in our community, much loved and respected, prepared with enthusiasm and delight for her third marriage. We thoroughly enjoyed the prenuptial social occasions, not so much to give her gifts since she had almost anything a bride could have desired, but for the pleasure of seeing that kind of confidence and anticipation the third time around! The sex ratio is so imbalanced by this stage in life that men number only about 70 percent as many as women. Since men also tend to down-marry in age, probably only about one half of the widows could expect to remarry the second or third time.

When One Plus One Equals Two Plus . . . N

Many restructured families involve children. The days are quite in the past when people were less apt to divorce if there were children. Three fourths of the remarried mothers have custody of their children. They face adjustment problems, the more so if there are several children from the former marriage. The quasi-comedy motion picture during the sixties became almost a documentary film as it referred to the children of a twice-married couple as *Yours, Mine, and Ours*. Most remarried parents admit that taking the step required more deliberation and planning when children were involved.

Children and stepchildren need to be included in the plans for a wedding, whether or not they are living with the remarrying parent. I know one widow who remarried after her children had gone off to college and simply wrote a letter (straight mail) informing them, then wondered why her children never endorsed (or condemned) the marriage or why they never made the new husband a second father! While obviously mature enough to accept such news if they were simply told what was going to happen, no doubt these college students felt that their relationship with the mother had preceded the one with her new husband and deserved better treatment. The younger the child of a remarrying mother, the better and more quickly he/she will adjust to the stepfather. In such cases, it may be that treating the young child as an understanding and adjusting being is also a matter of integrity and honesty. There is no reason to expect a near-grown child to accept the stepfather as a father; better to hope for friendship and respect.

Jessie Bernard found in her 1971 study that two thirds of the divorced men and 56 percent of the divorced women who remarried developed genuine affection for the children of their spouse. Only about 5 percent of the remarried persons rejected their stepchildren. Even when the couple have their own children, remarried persons appear to try to provide equal treatment and affection for all the children. If, in the courtship process, almost as much attention is given to winning the confidence of the children as in wooing the parent, half the battle may be won in starting the family as well as the marriage aright. It seems almost irrefutable to say that similar child-rearing values are more crucial to good adjustment even than those relating to the use of money, the choice of a house or of a church.

There is considerable evidence that remarriage is not harmful to children. It is not uncommon that unless carefully included they can at first feel rejected by both natural parent and stepparent alike. Adjustment seems to come more easily and readily to a stepfather than to a stepmother, though the negative stereotype of the stepmother has been grossly exaggerated. Any child will naturally try to manipulate a situation to his/her own benefit, whether with natural or stepparents. The wise mother or stepmother learns by experience the proper blend of discipline and affection. The rewards of patience and firmness can be unbelievably great!

"If At First You Don't Succeed . . ."

Was Browning right when he concluded, " 'Tis better to have loved and lost than never to have loved at all"? Does one defeat in marriage give you important experience and better odds for the second time around? Well, not necessarily, if we can believe most of the statistics and research on the American institution of marriage. One sociologist, Paul Landis has estimated that 50:50 chances of success can be expected in marriage when a single woman is thirty years old, a widow is thirty-three and a divorcee is forty-five. Whether this prediction is absolutely accurate or not, there seems to be little doubt that remarriage for the divorcée is more risky than marriage is for the never-married or widowed woman.

Women remarry for many of the same reasons that they marry—love, social expectations, security, companionship. If the second marriage endures and is happy, give the credit to personal maturity, tolerance, flexibility, tact, determination, and religious compatibility, just as in a first marriage. Unfortunately, experience and defeat do not always teach one to accept blame, to act tolerantly, or to solve problems. When questioned about the obstacles they faced in their second marriage, women most often mentioned their feelings of inadequacy in the skills of marriage, the fear that they had a tendency to choose mates poorly, worry over whether they might still be in love with their first husband, and the pressures from various friends and family to remarry. They were also quick to admit that they were sure that some stresses were in this remarriage that were not in their first marriage.

What we have been saying is that divorcees are more apt to remarry and also to divorce than single women and widows. If a second marriage does not succeed, usually it is a shorter one than even the first marriage. While those who make a second marriage work do so because *they* work hard at it, it seems that those who are really divorce-prone tend to give up after a rather short remarriage. There would seem to be an obvious connection between the widows' slower and more deliberate move toward remarriage and their more successful or durable experiences in it. The lowest divorce rates among remarrieds involve two widowed people or a widowed person married to a single person. This may be due to the facts that a widow's children are apt to be grown and out of the home, that the couple is nearer retirement, and that financial matters are more secure.

There are no pat recipes for blending the perfect remarriage, but here are some suggestions from one who has observed a number of very good ones:

Remarriage, like first marriage, depends not so much on picking exactly the right mate, but in attempting to be exactly the right mate. A lot of marriages which appeared at the outset to be "made in heaven" with just the right partners hopelessly fail because each one tried to go exactly halfway . . . and no further.

No relationship can be equalitarian; humans are not created equal in all areas of behavior. It is more important to strive for equity and mutual satisfaction. The power structure of any marital relationship must be like a see-saw—each partner yields or controls the balance of power in turn and occasionally the two are eye-to-eye with four feet on the ground and sharing the balance of power. Two mates who have each been "head" of their household have no need to compete for headship in all areas.

Bernard Grasset said, "To love is to stop comparing." This is a truism for a good remarriage; for there is no person who ever takes another's place or, for that matter, excels all other possible mates in every way.

Love Story was wrong . . . love is wanting to say you are wrong when you are! Love *is* being sorry and being able to say so. The greatest sin of omission in any relationship begins with the assumption that one you love *knows* you are sorry, you are forgiving, you are appreciative without having to hear it from you!

The secret of success for communicating in marriage is knowing how much and how little to verbalize. Women have been accused of overtalking a situation; men have been accused of undertalking—once they state their position, their ears stop up! All of us need to learn to talk through a problem or situation without retalking it, or "talking it to death!"

The chain of marriage is so heavy that it takes two to carry it and a third to guide–God. No marriage can be sublime without the spiritual adhesives; no marriage can be hopeless that begins and continues with spiritual unanimity.

Suggested Books on Remarriage

Baer, Jean. *The Second Wife*. New York: Doubleday, 1972.

Freda, Dorothy M. *Love the Second Time Around: the Divorcée's and Widow's Guide to Love, Laughter, and Living*. Laddin Press, 1969.

Grossman, Bruce C. and Hiebert, William T. "Preparation for Remarriage," *The Single Parent*. XIV (April, 1971) 31-32.

Martin, John R. *Divorce and Remarriage*. Scottsdale, Pa.: Herald Press, 1973.

McKain, Walter C. *Retirement Marriage*. University of Conn.: 1969.

Tybring, Jane B. "Remarriage: Parenting Someone Else's Children," *The Single Parent*. XVII (June, 1974) 19-20,27.

Epilogue

The tale of Eve, either with or without Adam, is still being chronicled. The future life-styles of her *and* her male hominid promise to be even more varied and rewarding, whether lived independently or together. Obviously their lives will be interwoven and related if they share marriage and a household or not. Insuring Eve's welfare socially and spiritually can only benefit Adam and his descendents. Toward that end this book has been written and dedicated to the more than one third who are unattached Eves and to those who love and are beloved by them.

Hopefully you have discerned the optimism and excitement of this writer. The only discontent I feel is that brevity of time and space required that I deal lightly or only by implication with many important areas in a single woman's life. But perhaps you have underlined again your confidence in the fact that the ongoing happiness and success of Eve (and Adam, of course) do not dwell in marital status, social circumstance, or even other people's actions. They are the fringe benefits of a full and mature life in which a woman accepts the premise that there are many kinds of satisfying human relationships and each kind may be enriched by suprahuman resources. I believe that in this paraphrase of the words of Paul the bachelor to another young single person he gave us a key to the good life, "For the gift of the eternal is that we need not live with fearfulness, but with love and courage and good mental health" (author's paraphrase).